Make Thou$ands on Amazon in 10 Hours a Week

How I Turned $200 into $40,000+ Gross Sales My First Year in Part-Time Online Sales

Revised December 2013

By Cynthia G. Stine

Learn more about the author's other works at:
http://amazon.com/author/cynthia

For Permission Requests, please contact the publisher at:

MyPromote Books
381 Casa Linda Plaza, Ste. 288
Dallas TX 75218
214-296-0984

ISBN 10: 149379163X
ISBN 13: 978-1493791637

First Printing -January 2012
Second Printing – December 2013
10 9 8 7 6 5 4 3 2 1

Acknowledgements

I am deeply grateful to my husband Tom and son Eric, who regularly put up with bags and boxes of merchandise all over the office and living room; and to Chris Green, who opened my eyes to the exciting world of retail arbitrage and who teaches me something new every time we talk.

I'd like to thank Susan Abrahamson, Lynn Rafter, Philip Stine, Lesley Hensell and Jean Sims for giving me helpful feedback and eagle-eyed edits. Tom Nadeau of IAM Graphic Design created the cover. Elbert Balbastro and Cherry Mae Davoc helped me layout the book, create my blog and Facebook fan page. Thank you all very much!

This book covers Cynthia Stine's experiences selling online using Amazon.com™'s "Fulfillment by Amazon™" or FBA program. Results may not be typical.

Please note: Some of the products and services mentioned in this book are for products and services for which the author may earn a referral fee or commission. Even though she earns a fee on some of her recommendations, she only recommends products and services that she has used or uses herself and that she feels will deliver good value and worth. Most services have a free trial period and many offer a no-questions-asked money-back guarantee.

TABLE OF CONTENTS

FOREWORD

People come up to Cynthia in stores, in checkout lanes and at book sales to ask what she's doing with her scanner and her piled-high baskets of goods...and she tells them. She's encouraged BigLots cashiers to start their own online Amazon.com™ businesses leveraging their employee discount at the store; she's gotten her dad and several colleagues and friends started with their own Amazon businesses; she's pitched several "friends of the library" groups to use Amazon's Fulfillment by Amazon™ (FBA) program to raise more money for their libraries than they can from just their annual book sale; and she's shared what she's learned with seller groups on Yahoo and Facebook. Her enthusiasm is infectious and she makes the business very easy to understand. She'll be the first to tell you that if she can do it, you can too.

As an entrepreneur and marketer for more than 25 years, Cynthia "gets" the concept of arbitrage and she knows her online customer, which makes her business efficient. Unlike eBay®, Amazon.com doesn't allow you a lot of license for clever descriptions or charming sales pitches – so how do you compete? This book will arm you with the strategies you need to make your own decisions for your business.

When I met Cynthia in 2010, her goals were modest – she wanted to pay for her son's private school while continuing with her day job. She turned a $200 investment in technology and supplies into a business that grossed more than $40,000 her first year – and that is on track to double this year. It beats the heck out of most part-time jobs and it's not pie-in-the-sky hype.

In this book, you'll learn about the tools, costs and – most importantly – strategies for making the most of your online business in the time you have available and with the financial resources you have available. She tells you exactly what she did and leads you by the hand through your first shipment to Amazon.com.

If you are interested in selling real products (books, toys, games, DVDs, CDs and more) online, I strongly suggest you read this book – and that you also _use_ it. Plan to have your first shipment off to Amazon.com by this time next week and in a year, you'll have your own success story to share.

Chris Green

Chris Green is the owner of ScanPower™, a company that gives Amazon.com sellers the tools they need to be successful and efficient in their Fulfilled-By-Amazon business. [www.ScanPower.com] His software was originally developed to help support his own thriving Amazon.com seller business. Now sellers around the country and in the U.K. use ScanPower List, ScanPower Mobile™ and ScanPower Repricer™ for an unfair competitive advantage. In addition to developing software, he has authored "Arbitrage: The authoritative guide on how it works, why it works, and how it can work for you." http://amazon.com/author/chris]

INTRODUCTION

Almost a year ago to the day of this writing, I was staring at my computer with dark-hollowed insomniac eyes as I tried to think my way out of my current situation. As a business owner for 16 years, I had ridden the financial roller coaster a few times, but I was out of ideas. I had moved my cheese, flipped over *Fish!* and tried several other smart, change-management programs.

Over the previous couple of years, I had sadly downsized my company several times until there was just me and then I moved home. My SBA loan taken out with such confidence in 2005, along with the line of credit from the bank and a credit card whose interest rate seemed to go up monthly, were costing me most of my diminished earnings every month. I hadn't paid myself in some time. I realized I was literally working for my creditors every month and it was depressing. I had gone from making about $180,000 in my workaholic heyday to making zero and still working my butt off.

To add to my mood, I was worried about my family's ability to pay our bills. We love our son's private school, where all the other kids are learning-challenged as he is, but the fees and other related medical costs are more than our monthly mortgage. My husband and I agreed that if I could somehow bring in an additional $1500 a month (net) to the family, we could handle the rest with austerity measures. $1500!!! It was such a small amount and yet so far away!

I had tried so hard to bring more business into my company, but all my potential clients had hunkered down with the economy. Some of my current clients were paying late, which was part of my problem, and a few simply closed, leaving unpaid bills.

I looked around my house and thought about selling stuff, but I didn't have much to sell. I'd gone on a big selling binge in the spring through Craigslist, which was not only a big hassle, but also time-consuming. That night I decided to take a different approach. It was actually something I'd learned from Tony Robbins' 30-day program that I completed in 1990.

I keyed into my laptop the parameters of an ideal part-time business. It needed to be:

* **Reliable** – I needed money to come in regularly without having to chase the check.
* **Flexible** – I wanted to spend as much time as possible with my son after school and I still had my day job working for the creditors.
* **Simple** – my current business was complicated enough.
* **Cheap** – I didn't have any money to work with.
* **Interesting** – It had to be something about which I felt genuine passion. I was burned-out dealing with the creditors and payment plans. I needed to feel good again.
* **Profitable** – $1,500-$2,000 a month after expenses. I needed a big bang for my buck— minimum wage returns weren't worth my time.
* **Sustainable** – I wanted something that was recession-resistant and something I could do over

and over again and get good results, unlike my current business.

For other people this list might be different, but my priorities shifted a lot when we adopted a teenager. Once I had my criteria firmly in mind, I went looking for this ideal part-time business. In addition to running a public relations firm, I'm also an independent publisher. Books have always been a passion of mine; I probably read 250+ books a year. I come from a family with two published authors and scholars, so publishing is in my blood. I looked at my bookshelves and an idea took hold. As much as I hated to part with my paper friends, maybe there was money to be made in selling them.

I went to the Amazon.com ("Amazon") website and was absolutely overwhelmed by what I saw when I clicked the "sell your book here" link. You may have realized this too – to list a book was a real pain! It would take days and days to list my books! In addition, a lot of them were worthless – people were selling them for a penny...what in the world?! Who makes money selling books for a penny?

Then I went to eBay®; maybe it would be better there. Plus, I had some designer kids' clothes that I thought would sell. eBay was even worse! Many of the fees were up-front, I had no clue what was a good starting point for an auction, and I had to write all my own listings. This would take forever. I spent hours reading the details on eBay's site about how to sell, special selling accounts... everything. I realized this business would never work for me. It was too much to learn, it was intimidating and I don't like the uncertainty of auctions. It seemed risky to me with all the upfront and mandatory fees. Having owned my own business(es) for 17 years, I knew I'd make mistakes in the beginning, and I needed to make money immediately from whatever I did.

I gave the children's clothes to a friend who is an eBay seller. We're sharing the profits after expenses and I'm thrilled–she's great at it and we both make money. In doing so, I used leverage – her time and expertise – and got rewarded for finding a super deal. This is the heart of arbitrage and the foundation for all sales-oriented business: Buy low, sell higher.

Next, I started looking at those "Make Money Selling Online!" books to see if someone had a better way. I found Nathan Holmquist's Selling on Amazon's FBA Program (http://bit.ly/NathanFREEbook) book and it changed everything for me. That book introduced me to Amazon's FBA (Fulfillment By Amazon) program, which was a revelation. My heart began to pound as I read the book in one sitting late at night. With FBA, I had the full might and power of Amazon behind me for a ridiculously low fee. What incredible leverage!

With FBA, you ship your books and other items for sale to an Amazon warehouse. Once the boxes get there, all your listings (conditions and pricing for your items) go live. Amazon stores your stuff in its warehouses. They take care of the money. They ship items to your customers super-fast and then they deposit a payment directly into your bank account for your portion every two weeks – like clockwork. If there's a problem, Amazon handles all the customer relations. It was like a dream come true- my entire wish list in one program.

When I dug into the numbers, I was excited. The fees for leveraging the number-one selling platform in the world are incredibly reasonable and manageable – and you pay Amazon's commissions after you sell something, not before.

In this book, I am going to use my actual numbers and experience to share with you what I did, what I learned and my strategies for success. I am by no means the most successful part-time FBA seller, but I am a real seller. If I can do it, you can too. Although your goals may be different from mine, I will show you how selling on Amazon works so you can reach those goals. My hope is that you will act on this book right away and begin realizing the benefits of more income immediately.

Today I sleep better at night. I've paid my son's tuition every month and we don't have to eat beans quite so often (although I like them just fine – I am a vegetarian). I'm looking forward to doubling or nearly doubling my income in Year 2, working the same number of hours as in Year 1. I'll tell you about that, too.

You picked up this book because you need money for something very important to you – otherwise you would not be looking so hard for an answer. If my story and my explanation of the FBA program and the tools and strategies I use appeal to you – please don't hesitate. Act immediately.

You don't need to know every single detail about Amazon to be successful. I've mentored many people who are learning as they go and who realized income right away. This book is a good starting point...please don't wait. You'll be glad you took action.

1

WHAT ARE YOU DOING?

I'm standing in line at BigLots with three overflowing shopping carts of toys, books, DVDs and baby items. Someone – often the cashier – asks, "What are you doing?" They have some interesting guesses like I run a daycare, I'm a teacher, earth mother of the year, or I work for some children's charity. They are surprised when I tell them I'm an Amazon seller and that I do this business part-time to pay for my son's private school. Even though they work at a discount store, the idea that what they sell is actually worth a lot more surprises them.

I'll show them my tiny scanner and the software application on my cell phone that makes it easy for me to shop. I'll give them the 30,000-foot view of Amazon's FBA program and how I don't have to store tons of inventory in my house or actually ship products to my customers. I keep it simple because it is simple.

I'll tell the minimum-wage cashier with the employee discount that "You could really do well in this business just by shopping your own store." I'll hand my business card to the curious person in line behind me with many questions and tell him to check out my blog. After a year of handing out cards, I've never gotten a call or email from them. It's sad, but typical.

That's how I know you are not typical. You are looking for extra money and you're willing to work for it. You've found this book and you're actually reading it. I commend you for this – you are already way ahead of the game. If you choose to act on what I tell you here, then you will also be way ahead of the majority of sellers on Amazon today. I don't say this because I'm a brilliant teacher with some gimmicky process, tip or trick. I say this because people who sell on Amazon using its FBA program are a still a very small percentage of the sellers on Amazon. They have a tremendous built-in competitive advantage. More on that later.

Before I tell you what I'm doing, I strongly suggest you spend five minutes and jot down exactly what you are doing. Why do you need the money? What will it let you do? What are your personal requirements for your business? Do you want to run it full-time or part-time? How will you measure your own success? Is it $1,000 a month? $3,000? $10,000?

Be specific and clear. For example, I am now making more than $1,500 a month with this business—the amount I actually needed to make it worth doing. I have new goals now, like family vacations and saving for retirement, but my driving reasons are the same. If I can't make $1,500 a month on average, then it is not worth my time and I need to do something else.

"What are you doing?" Over the past three years I've had friends and family ask me this question a lot. Because they know me, they know this is a serious business even though it is part-time. I'm a serial entrepreneur who has started and sold businesses. My entire 25+-year career, in one form or another has been spent helping my clients sell products and services and build their businesses.

Some of the people I told got a gleam in their eye and jumped into the business for themselves. I suddenly found myself helping them out in a haphazard, on-demand way. I created a PowerPoint which I walked people through. They generously gave me their feedback and asked questions...lots of questions.

That's how this book came about. I wanted to help in an organized way, and I wanted a way to answer the questions that everyone asks about the business. I've structured this book to answer the Top Eight Questions I hear the most:

1. **Can I really make money selling stuff on Amazon?**
2. **How do you do it?**
3. **What can I sell on Amazon?**
4. **Is it hard to find inventory?**
5. **Does it take a lot of time?**
6. **What do I need to make it work?**
7. **How much does it cost to get started?**
8. **Where can I get help?**

This book is based on my experience and the experiences of my family and friends in the business who shared some of their stories with me. It is by no means the be-all and end-all on this topic. In fact, I share the books, blogs and resources that I used and still use regularly to grow my business. I'm learning all the time from other Amazon sellers, which is part of the fun of this business. This book is also not a comprehensive omnibus of every possible tool and product out there for FBA sellers. I talk about what I know. For other products, I refer people to the extremely active and generous forums and groups out there for FBA sellers.

Although others have written books containing the many tools, tips and techniques from online sellers and those who sell to online sellers, I found these books to be very distracting and overwhelming in the beginning. I looked at many different technology solutions before choosing what I use today. I spent weeks reading and researching – I wish I'd had this book to learn from myself.

What I suggest for you is to follow the guidelines in this book, sell, and get some money in your pocket and experience under your belt. Then, if you want to explore all the many permutations of online selling, you will do it from a position of knowing what works. It will be much easier for you to determine how you want your business to grow and what kinds of products interest you the most.

Most people who start this business do it like I did it – with very few resources. For that reason, I focus on the basics. I talk about what you need immediately and what can wait. I started with $200. Everything I've bought or done in my business since then has been funded directly by my business. Even if you have more up-front cash to start, I recommend making your business pay for itself. I don't advocate going into debt.

What I hope for you is that this book allows you to make a decision – Is selling on Amazon for me? —and gives you the information you need to act on it right away. Every person I've told about this business who acted on it within a week has been successful – every one of them. You can be too. I may sound a little rah-rah here, but I'm not writing this book to sell it. I'm writing this book to help people change their financial situations and – by extension – their lives. If you are in a dark place as I was looking at bills you can't pay, I want to encourage you.

I'm an overextended mom and wife with limited resources. If I can do this, you can do this. You'll read real-world stories about a retiree looking for a certain amount of money to pay off some bills but not so much that he loses his retirement benefits; an under-employed consultant who needed to smooth the increasingly volatile income peaks and valleys with a reliable source of additional income; and a teacher wanting to make some extra money for the holidays.

I'll also include some great advice given to me by my mentor in this business, Chris Green. He has been an online seller for years on eBay and Amazon and was one of the first to join Amazon's FBA program. Even though he now also sells FBA software solutions for other resellers, he is still a top Amazon FBA seller who "walks the walk" every day. He makes more in a month as an Amazon seller than many people make in a year.

I've created a highly detailed Table of Contents so it will be easy for you to go to the information that is most important to you – and to return later when you are preparing your first shipment. At the end of most chapters, I suggest Take Action! steps to help you get started. In Chapter 4 and at the very end of the book is a master checklist of all the Action steps in one place.

Also, please note that technology changes faster than I can update this book. Amazon, ScanPower and other companies I mention in the book are constantly improving their offerings and changing their links and processes. For these reasons, all links are kept updated at my free membership site: http://www.makethousandsupdates.com. Please go there for the latest news and book updates.

TAKE ACTION!

1. Take a few minutes to list your personal criteria and goals for your Amazon business.
2. Plan how many hours you can devote to your business this week and commit the time toward getting your first shipment out. Write it in your calendar and keep the appointment with yourself.
3. Read the rest of the book.

2

CAN I REALLY MAKE MONEY SELLING ON AMAZON?

Do you think selling on Amazon is only for big companies? When I first learned about FBA, I heard several horror stories from people who had tried to sell on Amazon and "didn't make any money" – depressing tales. Because people also seemed to be more familiar with the eBay model, I got questions about whether I had a big enough garage or if I was warehousing my inventory off-site. Or how I figured shipping costs...that kind of thing. Several people told me they hadn't considered selling online because they didn't have the space for storing inventory.

The beauty of Amazon's FBA program – detailed in the next chapter – is that I don't have to worry about any of those things. I let logistics superstar Amazon take care of those details. To answer the question of whether or not I actually make money selling on Amazon, I'll share with you my first-year numbers.

Year One By The Numbers

- Gross sales $41,523.42
- Net $18,242.80

(Includes holiday sales below)
- Hours per month   40 (approx.)
- Earned per hour $38
- Holiday sales $6,387.64[1] (net)
- Initial start-up costs $200

It is like turning straw into gold. In the course of a year, I turned approximately $200 into $18,000+. The gross sales number represents the actual dollar amount of everything I sold.

The net figure is the amount that went into my bank account from Amazon—it's the net after paying all of Amazon's fees (commission, warehouse fee and $39.99 per month to be an Amazon Pro Seller), all my shipping costs, and the cost for ScanPower List, ScanPower Mobile and ScanPower Repricer. (I listed my actual dates and deposits for you below.) What it does not include is the actual cost for my shipping boxes, tape, inventory, office supplies, portable scanner, inventory acquisition and some books I bought in the beginning about selling using Amazon's FBA Program. My best estimate for these costs is approximately $6,000 of which most was for inventory acquisition. Thus, my actual net was closer to $12,000 for Year 1.

Again, considering that I had about $200 to start with, I'm thrilled with these numbers. All my inventory acquisition and additional equipment was paid for out of the business as I went along. I was able to take out roughly $1,000 a month to pay for my son's private school and I'm in a terrific position for Year 2.

---

[1] From November 14, 2010 – February 6, 2011.

I didn't necessarily spend 40 hours every month on the business —that's an average. I tend to work in "bursts." As you will see, there are months in which I spent very little time on the business because I was busy with my family or my day business or whatever. Other months, I spent more time. I spent a lot of time the first three weeks in December, for example, because sales were terrific and I wanted to feed the demand. I made approximately 33% of my total year's income during the holiday season.

First Year Payouts From Amazon

Dates	Amount
9/5/2010 – 9/19/2010	(-$56.10[2])
9/19/2010 – 10/3/2010	$155.69
10/3/2010 – 10/17/2010	$334.21
10/17/2010 – 10/31/2010	$450.47
10/31/2010 – 11/14/2010	$88.15
11/14/2010 – 11/28/2010	$480.02
11/28/2010 – 12/12/2010	$762.21[3]
12/12/2010 – 12/26/2010	$2,135.41
12/26/2010 – 1/9/2011	$1,244.75
1/9/2011 – 1/23/2011	$833.61
1/23/2011 – 2/6/2011	$931.64
2/6/2011 – 2/20/2011	$250.00
2/20/2011 – 3/6/2011	$498.48
3/6/2011 – 3/20/2011	$1,506.35
3/20/2011 – 4/3/2011	$1,634.93
4/3/2011 – 4/17/2011	$1,259.51
4/17/2011 – 5/1/2011	$955.45
5/1/2011 – 5/15/2011	$625.30
5/15/2011 – 5/29/2011	$251.69

[2]This was my first shipment to Amazon and represented the UPS cost.
[3]I bought my first toys in early December

5/29/2011 – 6/12/2011	$121.87
6/12/2011 – 6/26/2011	$135.21
6/26/2011 – 7/10/2011	$454.08[4]
7/10/2011 – 7/24/2011	$372.17
7/24/2011 – 8/7/2011	$376.76
8/7/2011 – 8/21/2011	$552.44
8/21/2011 – 9/4/2011	$975.97
9/4/2011 – 9/18/2011	$912.53
TOTAL:	$18,242.80

As they say in all the diet ads, your actual results may vary. I find that when I'm able to spend time, my numbers go up. Right now, I'm sending in big shipments every week. It is book sale season in my area, so many of those shipments are books along with some toys. Starting in October, I'll focus heavily on toys for the holiday season.

In Year 1, I was constrained by my finances. I couldn't afford to buy any inventory in the beginning so I used my own book and media collection as inventory. This is a terrific way to start and I recommend it for the following reasons:

- **Sunk Costs:** Your costs for this inventory were sunk long ago, so your effective cost today is $0.
- **Mistake-Friendly:** Like your first car, your first few shipments to Amazon are where you will make most of your mistakes. You might as well make them on used books and media you already own.
- **Easy Testing:** You can test pricing and ranking with very little risk to you. Want to see how long it.

---

[4]We were on vacation for these two weeks and I didn't have to do a thing for my business

takes to sell a book that's ranked at 1 million in terms of how fast it sells? At 10,000? You probably have some on your shelf right now. I have a few books still in Amazon's warehouse from my first shipment last September where I've learned that over 2 million is too high in books, for example.

- **Step-by-Step Learning:** You don't have to learn everything all at once. In other words, you can focus on scouting and shopping later after you are comfortable with pricing and shipping items.
- **Pay Off Start-up Costs Faster:** The money you gain from these items can cover your start-up costs and help you acquire new inventory.

In Year 2, I expect to *more than double* what I made in Year 1 without necessarily spending any more time on the business. Why is this?

- **Latent Inventory**: I currently have $37,829.50 in inventory (October 2011). In other words, if all those items sell for the price I want, I'll make $37,829.50 gross. That's almost as much as I made all last year. This gross sales number does not even include my last two shipments, which were quite large and represent an additional $5,000+ in latent inventory. This is a heck of a lot better than the $0 I started with a year ago.
- **Holidays:** Last year I didn't have much money to spend on toy inventory and hadn't even sold toys until December – just books, DVDs and CDs. This year I plan to have lots of toys for sale starting in mid-to-late October. My goal is to gross $15,000-$20,000 in the holiday season alone.

- **Momentum:** This year I'm smarter, faster and better prepared. Each batch of inventory I acquire is more and more profitable and efficient in terms of money earned per hour.
- **More $ for Inventory**: I've been saving up.
- **Learning Curve:** I know so much more about the business this year that it enables me to buy more confidently and successfully. While I'm sure I will still make mistakes, I will make fewer of them.

In sharing my numbers, I hope you can see that selling on Amazon through FBA is no "get-rich-quick" scheme – <u>and</u> success is attainable. If you could be $12,000 richer by the end of a year, would that be meaningful to you? There are people in this business who do much, much better than I do. They have more time and they had more money for start-up costs and inventory. It really is as simple as that. If you can buy more, you can make more, faster.

My Dad wanted to make $13,000 over the holidays his first year. He achieved this because he had more money for inventory than I did my first year.

We will talk more about how I actually did it in the next chapter.

TAKE ACTION!

1. If you've not already, determine your minimum financial goals for this business. Write them down.
2. Determine how much you will need to make per hour (on average) to make this worthwhile for you and write this number down.

3. Determine how much money you have to invest in your business and write this number down. If it is only $200, then your progress will be slower but steady. If you have more for inventory, it will be faster.
4. Based on what you've read, is this business of interest to you so far? Why or why not? Jot down your thoughts so you can look at them when you're done with the book.
5. Read the rest of the book.

3

How Do You Do It?

The beating heart of my business is Amazon's FBA program. Here's how I do it:

* I acquire inventory at cheap prices – see Buy Low, Sell High later in this chapter for more.
  * I use an online software program developed by ScanPower [up-to-date links are kept at: http://www.makethousandsupdates.com] to list the condition and price of my items. This program also prints off a small label with a barcode that I put on the back of my item.
* I pack my boxes and ship them to Amazon's warehouses. I get to use Amazon's incredibly discounted shipping rate.
* At the warehouse, the items are scanned and stored for me. The minute they are scanned, my listing goes live on Amazon's site. Some of my items have sold so quickly that they never made it off the warehouse floor into storage.
* When my item sells, Amazon handles the credit card transaction, ships the product and takes care of any customer service issues for me.

- Every two weeks (26 times a year), Amazon deposits money directly into my bank account. They take out any shipping charges, commissions and warehouse storage fees first, so the money deposited is my net.
- Depending on my financial needs, I keep half and spend the other half on new inventory.

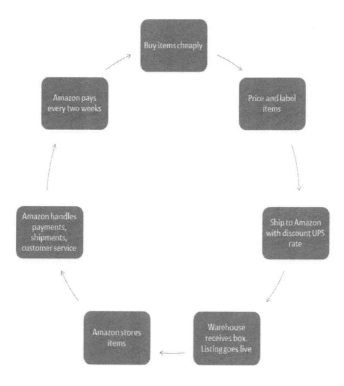

Figure 1: My online business using Amazon's FBA Program

That's it! Of course there are details, but if you understand this, you understand why this business is so powerful for small businesses like mine...and yours. You find good stuff to sell, and Amazon takes care of the rest.

Amazon has easy-to-understand information about how its program works. Not all of these links will work on the Kindle. Check http://www.makethousandsupdates.com if these don't work:

- How it works – http://amzn.to/FBAprogram
- FBA guidelines – http://amzn.to/fbaguidelines
- How it works in the warehouse video – http://amzn.to/warehousevideo
- FBA fees – http://bit.ly/FBAfees
- Get started with Amazon FBA video – http://amzn.to/fbagetstarted
- Fulfillment by Amazon manual – http://amzn.to/fbamanual

Of these videos, Get Started is best viewed after you've signed up. Otherwise it won't make much sense. It is largely aimed at current merchant sellers who want to use Amazon's FBA program.

Be sure to bookmark the Fulfillment by Amazon Manual and FBA Guidelines. They answer a lot of questions and few Amazon sellers even know these resources exist.

What You Need to Know to Get Started

For those who want to dive in and get started, go to **Chapter 4.** I have a checklist of the things you need to do in the first week or so to get your business in place and prepare to send your first box to Amazon. Come back to this chapter later when you want to understand how the fees and pricing work.

Fees

The biggest mistakes people make when first using the FBA program are usually around pricing and fees – and you can't price effectively if you don't understand your fees. Bear with me through this section – I'll pull it all together at the end so you can price smartly. Also, be aware that Amazon changes its fees from time to time. The fee structure will probably stay the same (i.e. the types of fees that Amazon charges) but some of the costs may go up. Be sure when you are creating your own pricing rules or guidelines that you use the most current Amazon fees which you can find in Amazon's Seller Central when you become a Pro Seller on Amazon.

If you don't want to read about the details behind the fees right now, jump ahead to where I have the bottom line on how the description of its fees affect my final paycheck.

Let me start by saying that Amazon makes the fees unnecessarily complicated, and I can't say that I understand their logic perfectly. What I have done is set up spreadsheets and rules for myself so I can make good buying decisions.

They are smart enough to realize their fees are complicated so they offer two tools for new sellers. One is an FBA Calculator (http://bit.ly/FBACalculator) that allows you to figure out the fees on an inventory item. The other is called Fee Preview in Seller Central. When you look at your inventory, it will show you to the far right of each item the fees that will be assessed if you sell that item at your chosen price. This is handy to have when you are repricing.

Amazon charges fees for:
* Shipment to the warehouse
* Order fulfillment
* Inventory storage
* Commissions/Selling on Amazon

Shipment to the warehouse is the cost of UPS® shipping. You get the benefit of Amazon's deeply discounted rate – about 25-to-50 cents a pound – and don't even have to pay any money up front. Amazon will take the fees out of your next deposit. If you remember my deposits from last year, the first one was actually a negative number. This is because I was paying for my shipment and had not yet sold enough to cover the cost. That was my only negative payment. Amazon took it out of my bank account.

Order fulfillment covers three fees:
* Handling Fee
* Pick and Pack
* Weight per pound

The handling fee for books and other media is only relevant if you use FBA to fulfill orders from other sites on which you're selling, like eBay or your own website. Because I don't sell on other sites, I've not included information in the book about this aspect of Amazon's FBA program. You can check it out here if you're interested. [http://amzn.to/multichannelFBA]. There is currently no handling fee for items sold on Amazon.

Pick and Pack is based on the size of your product. It is $1 (for small and large standard-sized items) or $4-$10 (for oversized items). Lastly, there is a weight-per-pound fee of 42 cents for small standard-size and 46 cents for large standard-size items up to 1 pound, 76 cents for 2 pounds and an additional 40 cents above 2 pounds. Weight per pound can sneak up on you when you're selling heavy textbooks.

Here's an example from Amazon of order fulfillment fees for a typical half-pound softcover book:

- **Weight**: 0.5 lb.
- **Dimensions**: 7.5" x 5.2" x 0.8"
- **Selling Price**: $10

Fee	Calculation	Amount
Order Handling	1 order x $0.00	$0.00
Pick & Pack	1 Unit x $1.00	$1.00
Weight Handling	0.5 lb. x $0.40	$0.46
Total		$1.46

Pick and Pack and Weight Handling vary by size of item as I mentioned before.

Here's an example from Amazon of order fulfillment fees for an oversized keyboard and mouse:

- **Weight:** 1.8 lb.
- **Outbound Shipping Weight:** 3 lb.
- **Dimensions:** 20.62" x 6.25" x 1.87"
- **Selling Price**: $70

Fee	Calculation	Amount
Order Handling	1 order x $0.00	$0.00
Pick & Pack	1 Unit x $4.00	$4.00
Weight Handling	1.8 lb. + 1 lb. packing materials	$1.37
Weight Handling Fee	.99 cents for first 2 lbs. and .38 cents for third lb.	
Total		**$5.37**

As you can see, the fees are less to sell a book than a keyboard. However, you can generally sell a keyboard for a lot more than a book.

Inventory Storage fees kick in one month after Amazon has received your item. If your item sells in less than a month, you won't pay any warehousing fee. I currently have more than 2,400 items at the warehouse and only paid $42 in storage fees last month. This means that my storage fees are less than 1% of my total inventory per month.

The last storage unit I rented for my day job cost me $85 a month for a 10'X10' unit, which wouldn't be nearly big enough for my current inventory. And I certainly didn't have a crew fulfilling orders for me. This is a tremendous advantage of Amazon's FBA program.

Amazon has detailed measurements and weights for every item available on their site. They use these measurements and weights to assess what you owe them – it doesn't matter how many Amazon warehouses you are actually using. Right now, for example, I have items warehoused in Texas, Indiana, Arizona, Tennessee and Pennsylvania.

Inventory fees are also seasonal. Amazon charges more for storage during the busy holiday season $.45 per cubic foot during the months of January-September and $.60 per cubic foot in October-December.

Using the paperback book in the previous example, you can see that it only costs 2.5 cents per month to store it after the first month, for most of the year. During the months of October-December, that book will cost a mere 3.4 cents to store. If that book is in inventory for 13 months (1 free month + 12 regular months), it will cost you **33 cents a year** in storage costs – a pittance.

At the end of my first year, I had several books in inventory from my very first shipment. These were experiments and part of my learning process. I have the choice now of leaving them there or having them removed by Amazon. Since this book is focused on getting you started, I'll cover removals – and other maintenance issues – in later writings. I also cover more advanced topics on my blog at: www.sellstepbystep.com where I have many posts about how to run your day-to-day business.

Commissions/Selling on Amazon is basically your listing fee. Unlike auction sites, you don't have to pay it until the item sells. This fee is 99-cents per item. If you are selling more than 40 items a month, then you'll want to upgrade to the Selling on Amazon Subscription Fee of $39.99 a month, which allows you unlimited sales for this one fee. In August 2011, I sold 204 items, which means my Selling on Amazon fee was approximately 20 cents an item. Upgrading makes you a Pro Seller on Amazon.

The other fees that are calculated under Selling on Amazon are commissions and variable closing fees. Amazon calls commissions referral fees and they vary according to category. I've printed the list here from Amazon's site. For the most part, I'm paying 15% commissions since I primarily sell books, toys, games, baby products, office products and media items.

See the next page for Amazon's referral fees.

Referral Fees

Product Type	Referral Fee Percentage
Baby Products (excluding baby apparel)	15%
Beauty	15%
Books	15%
Camera and Photo	8%
Consumer Electronics	8%
DVD	15%
Electronics Accessories	15% (minimum $1)
Grocery & Gourmet Food	15%
Health and Personal Care	15%
Home & Garden (including Pet Supplies)	15%
Kindle Accessories	25%
Music	15%
Musical Instruments	12%
Office Products	15%
Personal Computers	6%
Software & Video Games	15%
Sports & Outdoors	15%
Tires & Wheels	10%
Tools & Home Improvement	12%
Toys& Games	15%
Video & DVD	15%
Video Game Consoles	8%
Any Other Products[5]	15%

---

[5]There are other categories on Amazon like automotive, clothing, jewelry, collectible books etc., but they are restricted so I did not list them here. You need special permission to sell in those categories.

Variable Closing Fee Schedule

Media Product Type	Variable Closing Fee
Books	$1.35
Music	$0.80
Videos (VHS)	$0.80
DVDs	$0.80
Video Games	$1.35
Video Game Consoles	$1.35
Software & Computer Games	$1.35

Variable Closing Fees are assessed for processing the order through Amazon. Think of it as the fee Amazon charges you for using its credit card processing system and for any customer support that might be needed for that item.

For media, they charge a flat fee (see above) per item. There is no variable closing fee on the sale of non-media products fulfilled using the Fulfillment by Amazon™ service. So while you'll pay a $1.35 variable closing fee for selling a computer game, you won't pay a variable closing fee on a Barbie doll. To be clear, what you will pay on the Barbie doll is the commission fee. For a $45 Barbie, that works out to $6.75. I know this is confusing. The most important thing to remember from this discussion of fees is that they exist. Even if you don't understand them, if you can allow for them in your pricing, you'll do fine. Amazon lists all fees on its site as well. Once you are a Pro Seller on Amazon, you can look them up in your Seller Central account under Help.

FEES: BRINGING IT ALL TOGETHER – HOW DO YOU KNOW YOU ARE MAKING A PROFIT?

Standing in front of a shelf of Barbie dolls or discounted bestseller books is not the time to calculate fees and profits. Early on, I devised some rules for myself that allow me to shop with confidence. I calculated fees and profits for a typical item in each category in which I sell, and then used it as my starting point. I know for how much I must sell an item to make it worthwhile.

The chart shows actual numbers from products I sold recently using fees current as of October 2013. PLEASE be sure that you are looking at the latest fees when you figure out your costs and profits in the future.

I estimated a per-unit cost (miscellaneous expenses) for boxes, tape, UPS pick-up fees, barcode labels, software subscriptions, etc. – the cost of doing business – based on the number of units I shipped to Amazon the month I created this chart.

I did not include taxes because I now buy most of my items sales tax free. Of course I do file taxes later, but my customers pay the sales taxes, not me. I simply file them. Amazon charges a small 2.9% of tax collected fee, but I don't include that in these calculations since many of my products sold are exempt from sales tax.

In the spreadsheet on the next page, you'll notice that I include the actual dollars that Amazon sent me, and I show my net after my other expenses. In the paperback example, I turned 10 cents into $3.38.

Of course, it is more fun and efficient to make $18.82 from a $2 investment like the textbook (see chart).

Lastly, I show you my personal minimum prices. When I'm at a book sale looking at paperbacks, for example, I take my minimum price; add the actual cost of a paperback at the sale (say 50 cents) and that is the smallest amount I must see on my scanner in order to buy the book. (The scanner shows the current offers for that product online – I'll talk more about the tools I use later).

If you look at the paperback book, you see that my out-of-pocket expenses are $2.70, not including the cost of the book. If I sell that book for $8 (assuming no cost for the book – if I already owned the book, let's say), then I'll make a $4 profit. Because I buy most of my books today, I need to subtract the acquisition cost from the $4.00 profit. If the book at the book sale is 50 cents, then I need to see a minimum of $6 selling price on my scanner to make it worthwhile to buy the book. In that case, I would make a profit of $1.90.

Many of the books I buy at book sales are selling online for $7 to $10 and up, which gives me a nice margin.

I prefer to see at least a $4 profit in my books. This is largely because I need to allow for competition. It is quite possible that I'll need to reprice before the book sells. I may list it for $7.99 but ultimately sell it for less. I've learned over time to leave in room in the book category. If I'm buying a book for $2 and selling it for $35.00, I have a lot more room to discount.

	Rhinoceros& Other Plays	Black Inventors	Biology
	Paperback Book	Hardback Book	Textbook
Actual sales price	$7.99	$10.99	$35.00
Amazon Fees			
- Commission	($1.20)	($1.65)	($5.25)
- FBA per-unit fee	($1.00)	($1.00)	($1.00)
- FBA weight-based fee	($0.46)	($0.76)	($3.76)
- Variable closing fee	($1.35)	($1.35)	($1.35)
TOTAL DEPOSIT FROM AMAZON:	$3.98	$6.23	$23.64
Acquisition cost	($0.10)	($1.00)	($2.00)
Other costs			
- Subscription fee $39.99/month	($0.20)	($0.20)	($0.20)

	Rhinoceros& Other Plays	Black Inventors	Biology
- Shipping estimate (to warehouse)	($0.25)	($0.50)	($2.50)
-1 month storage fee	($0.025)	($0.035)	($0.06)
- Miscellaneous expenses	($0.06)	($0.06)	($0.06)
TOTAL OTHER EXPENSES	($0.635)	($1.80)	($4.82)
NET PROFIT (rounded):	$3.35	$5.34	$18.82
MINIMUM OUT-OF-POCKET EXPENSES (not incl. acquisition cost or commission fee):	$2.70	$3.26	$7.23
MY PRICING MINIMUMS FOR THE CATEGORY:	$6.99	$7.50	$10.00

[Don't forget to add your actual product cost to the pricing minimum when scouting.]

MORE EXAMPLES:

	Johnny Carson	Coffee Maker	Hulk Plush Doll	Diaper Disposal Sack
	VHS	Kitchen	Toy	Baby
Actual sales price	$10.99	$94.85	$33.99	$9.99
Amazon Fees				
- Commission	($1.65)	($14.23)	($3.75)	($3.74)
- FBA per-unit fee	($1.00)	($4.00)	($4.00)	($1.00)
- FBA weight-based fee	($0.46)	($4.03)	($.99)	($0.42)
- Variable closing fee	($0.80)	$.0.00	$0.00	$0.00
- Order Handling	$0.00	($1.00)	($1.00)	($1.00)
TOTAL:	$7.08	$71.59	$22.90	$6.07
Out-of-pocket cost	($0.25)	($27.20)	($7.99)	($1.49)
Other costs				
- Subscription fee $39.99/month	($0.20)	($0.20)	($0.20)	($0.20)
- Shipping estimate (to warehouse)	($0.25)	($5.00)	($.50)	($0.12)
-1 month storage fee	($0.02)	($0.44)	($0.05)	($0.025)
- Miscellaneous expenses	($0.06)	($0.06)	($0.06)	($0.06)
NET PROFIT:	$6.30	$38.69	$14.10	$4.18

	Johnny Carson	Coffee Maker	Hulk Plush Doll	Diaper Disposal Sack
MINIMUM OUT-OF-POCKET EXPENSES (not incl. acquisition cost or commission fee):	$2.79	$14.73	$6.80	$2.42
MY PRICING MINIMUMS FOR THE CATEGORY:	$6.00	$30.00	$14.00	$5.00
[Don't Forget to add your actual acquisition costs to these numbers when scouting]				

If you look at the Hulk Plush toy, you see that I need to see a price of at least $14 plus my acquisition cost to even consider the toy. In actuality, I like better margins than that on toys and baby items due to their extreme price fluctuations and the fact that Amazon tends to be aggressive in its own pricing in these categories. I'm also paying more out of pocket, so I want a higher return for my inventory investment. For non-media categories, I want to see 3X or better on my scanner, or three times the acquisition cost. For the Hulk toy that cost $8, I needed to see $24 on the scanner to even consider it. But because it was oversized, I knew my costs would be higher.

Rather than doing the math in my head at the store, I relied on my scouting tool to do the math for me. I could look at my smartphone and quickly realize that the Hulk doll was a good deal. I cover scouting and pricing in more detail later in the book and show how my tools combined with my personal minimums help me make fast decisions at the store.

PAYMENTS

This is the most exciting section of the book: payment! When you set up your account on Amazon, you have the option of direct deposit every two weeks. Here are just a few things to know:

* Tax ID number: If you don't have a business set up yet or a business banking account, set that up first. It will make accounting easier for you later.

* Escrow: You won't get paid everything you are owed in the beginning. The first two weeks Amazon builds up an escrow account of your money and holds on to it. This escrow is to cover future shipping charges, refunds and other activities for which they may need to charge you down the road. Once you prove yourself and build up funds in your account, they'll release the money.

* Four-day lag: It takes four days for the payment to get into your bank account from Amazon. If they distribute on a Sunday, you get paid on a Thursday.

* Taxes: You are expected to pay your own sales taxes. They have an option where they collect your taxes from your customers for you for a small fee. To my mind, this is a no-brainer and I've signed up— calculating my state taxes is one less thing I have to worry about. I use a program called TaxJar (see Resources at the end of the book) that takes

data from Amazon and tells me what I need to file and pay in each state where I'm registered.

* Reports: Amazon keeps real-time reports online of all your sales transactions, their fees and your net profits. They also send you an email when a payment is sent to your bank account.

AMAZON REPORTS

Amazon provides a dizzying list of reports for you to manage your business. You can access them through your Amazon Seller account once it is set up. These include:

* Inventory – everything relating to your inventory. From the inventory page, you can go to your shipping queue, download inventory reports, change prices, delete items from inventory and more.
* Payments – shows sales you have made for any given period, who bought your items and from what state. This is where you will keep track of your pending (and past) payments from Amazon. In addition, you can look at individual transactions to see Amazon's fees and your net profit.
* Amazon Selling Coach – covers ways you can improve your sales and statistics on your inventory.
* Business – gets into the nitty-gritty of your sales by date, by SKU (your personal identifier for each product), by site views and more. I rarely use these, given the short amount of time I have to focus on this business every week.

I cover specific Amazon reports in more detail in my blog posts. What you need to know at this point is that Amazon keeps track of absolutely everything that happens on its site. If you have a question about your inventory, there's likely already an answer in one of those reports.

KNOW YOUR CUSTOMER

FBA sellers have access to different customers than other Amazon sellers, also known as merchant sellers. In particular, your target customer is the Amazon Prime Member. Amazon Prime is a program that gives members free two-day or greatly reduced one-day shipping on all orders, free video downloads, free Kindle lending library, and more. Prime members even have a different view of the site when they visit and frequently search for items based on whether or not they are Prime eligible. They don't even see competitive merchant offers – a huge advantage for FBA sellers. If you are not a Prime member now, you may want to join at some point as a way to understand your customer. The cost is $79 a year.

Here are the characteristics of Amazon Prime members:

* Impatient
* Internet savvy
* Frequent online shoppers
* Loyal – will often use the site without checking other sites
* Fans of Amazon's shipping and customer service
* Price-resistant – buyers who will pay a premium for better and faster service

- Will pay more for the peace of mind of working with Amazon
- Will buy from multiple categories, not just media

In short, Prime members are Amazon's biggest spenders and most frequent users. Amazon estimates that Prime members spend on average $500 more per year than typical site visitors. They are the most valuable customers on Amazon's site and now they are your customers. When you list your item as Fulfillment by Amazon, Prime members know that their product will be shipped directly from the warehouse to them by Amazon, rather than from a merchant (third-party) seller. The item will also be covered by Amazon's famous "A-to-Z" satisfaction guarantee and world-class customer service, neither of which is the case when buying from merchant sellers.

This advantage is so powerful that even non-Prime members will be drawn to the FBA seller. Last month, 44% of my sales were to Prime buyers, which is not surprising. What is astounding is that 56% of my customers were not Prime buyers! Why is this so amazing? I usually charge more than the merchant sellers, and I rarely have the lowest-priced offer. My customers are so loyal to Amazon and pleased with its service that they will pay a premium for it.

Another reason that so many non-Prime members may have been attracted to my merchandise is the Amazon Buy Box. As an FBA seller, I am eligible for and frequently listed in the Buy Box, which means that mine is the first offer a visitor sees. They can click on my offer, have the item paid for through Amazon's 1-click payment system and be done with the order in less than a minute.

Amazon only sells new merchandise, which immediately puts your used books and media at an advantage. Now the Prime buyer can get used media expedited the same way as with new.

As I mentioned earlier, when a Prime member logs in, their site is a little bit different. Offers eligible for free shipping are highlighted in their searches ahead of merchant-fulfilled items. Think about that. Even if a merchant seller is offering a lower price than you, your item will come up first because you are the FBA seller. This is a huge competitive advantage! Certainly with a few more clicks a Prime buyer can look at all the offers if desired, but most of them do not – they prefer to buy Prime for the reasons previously cited.

We'll talk more about this later under pricing strategies.

LEVERAGE TECHNOLOGY

The beauty of this business is that it is technology-enabled. You don't need a warehouse or a lot of new equipment to get going. If you already have a home office and/or a computer, you have most of what you need to get started. In this section, I'll identify the tools I use. Later in the book, I will walk you through step-by-step until your first shipment is on its way to Amazon.

You can find links to all the products I use on my website on the Supplies for your FBA Business page and inside my free membership site.

Inventory Tracking and Posting Software – I use ScanPower [https://unity.scanpower.com/register], an online subscription program that makes it easy for me to prepare my listings for Amazon, print off barcode labels for my items and ship to the correct warehouse. I create unique SKUs (stock-keeping units) that help me keep track of my items, including where and when I bought them. The first two weeks are a free trial. If you bought my eBook and use [https://unity.scanpower.com/register], you'll get an extra two free weeks – an entire month total – to try it. Follow the additional instructions that came with your welcome email after buying the book. ScanPower is the first service I used for listing my personal library of books.

If you go to http://www.makethousandsupdates.com, I've listed links to ScanPower videos for you. In addition, please remember that technology changes frequently so if the registration link above is obsolete, I'll keep the updates page in my membership site current.

USB Scanner – You will need some kind of handheld scanner that plugs into your computer to read the ISBN#s and UPC codes on the back of your books and other inventory. Buy a cheap one for $25 or less to sit by your computer. If you are low on start-up funds, just get ScanPower and a USB scanner to process your home library of books, DVDs, CDs, VHS tapes, software, audio books, etc. Sell stuff from your family and neighbors (share profits with them). As your items sell, you'll be able to afford more tools and inventory.

Label Printer – ScanPower generates small labels with your unique barcode that you will put on the back of your merchandise (covering the ISBN#). If you have a label printer at your desk, you can quickly print the label, put it on the product and drop it in a box. If you are short on funds, you can wait to buy a label printer because Amazon will create labels for you that print on 8.5"x11" sheets of stickers. This service is free but it is also more time-consuming because you have to match labels to items, which can be a pain if you have more than 10-20 unique items. When you are ready to buy a label printer, get either a LabelWriter or a Zebra. I have the LabelWriter 450 Turbo, which costs about $70 on Amazon. I've also seen them for sale (used of course) more cheaply on Craigslist.

Portable Database – When scouting for New inventory, you need the freshest possible information to make a good decision. I currently use ScanPower's Mobile app on my smartphone. It consists of two parts: an application that runs on smartphones (phones with Android™ operating system and iPhone® phones), iPod touch® or iPad®; and a tiny Bluetooth™ laser-scanner that reads barcodes and transmits the numbers into ScanPower Mobile on your phone.

ScanPower Mobile shows you FBA offers as well as merchant sellers. In addition, it connects real-time to Amazon so the data is current as of that minute. See my updates page in my free membership site for links to videos from ScanPower on how it works.

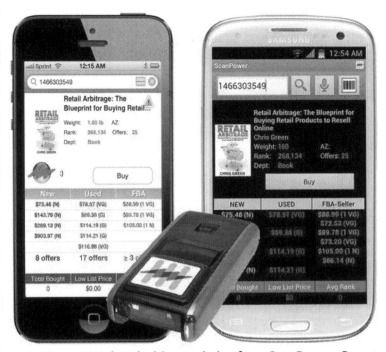

Image reprinted with permission from ScanPower. ©2013

As you can see, the data is neatly organized for quick decisions. At a glance I know that I want this book. The letters after the price tell me the condition. VG= Very Good, N= New, and so on. I compare the condition of the book I want to buy against the condition of the other (same) books offered for sale. You can't see it clearly on this picture, but ScanPower Mobile gives you the net for every price. If you see the $88.99 (VG) offer up above on the right, the $72.53 underneath it is the net price. That means if I sell the book for $88.99, Amazon will deposit $72.53 into my bank account. The net includes all of Amazon's fees and commissions. It does NOT include my out-of-pocket cost for the book, nor does it cover my packing and shipping costs. I have to mentally subtract those costs when I'm looking at the net figure.

This alone is a tremendous advantage to me as a shopper – no having to figure out commissions, weights, shipping costs and fees in my head. ScanPower Mobile will do it for me.

The weight of the book also figures into my consideration (remember my chart with the paperback, hardback and textbook) as does the Amazon department in which it will be listed. Be sure to look at the department pulled up by ScanPower Mobile before deciding to buy. The listing department for books is obvious, but the listing department for some items, like calendars, isn't clear and you have to look at the category carefully.

For example, you can find calendars in both the Books and Office Supplies departments, and the rankings in each department are very different. Software, video games and DVDs can sometimes be found in books, sometimes in toys, sometimes in video games. If you don't know the appropriate category, you can make a mistake and buy something that will take months or years to sell. ScanPower Mobile gives you the information you need to make shopping much smarter.

Another advantage of ScanPower Mobile – one that has opened up my business tremendously – is the fact that it will give you prices for virtually any item with a barcode. Now, in addition to books, I also sell toys, games, home goods, pet supplies, baby items and more with complete confidence. I find the financial returns are often better with these items than with books. With ScanPower Mobile, I am limited only by my curiosity.

The day I got my Scanfob® and ScanPower Mobile (December 3, 2010) is the day I officially became an Amazon seller rather than an online bookseller. Because the fob is tiny, I wear it around my neck with a lanyard so I don't have to worry about dropping it or losing it.

I also use a wristband to carry my smartphone so I can use both my hands as I shop. I scan, look at the smartphone on my wrist, decide and go to the next item.

When I shop, I wear a fanny pack so I'm completely hands-free. In my pack, I carry tissues (you wouldn't believe how dusty a book sale can be), a permanent marker with a fine tip, my checkbook/credit cards and a backup battery for my phone and Scanfob. The battery is essential for marathon shopping days – I can plug in my depleted phone or Scanfob and keep shopping. I have never used up the battery pictured on the Supplies page of my blog, it's a humdinger (RAVPower Element 10400mAh External Battery Pack).

While not high tech, another item you will need at some point is a dolly for carrying book boxes –I have several. One is a large, industrial dolly that I bought at Sam's Club for about $80. It can be pulled as a flatbed cart or used in the upright position. It carries up to 900 pounds and helps me move heavy boxes around my house (I've stacked nine on it before) and out to the car or front porch. I also have a smaller fold-up dolly that is great for carting two or three boxes around a book sale. It is small, maneuverable and beats the heck out of carrying a heavy bag. I got my small dolly for $25 at Sam's Club and have since seen a similar one for $20 at BigLots.

In one of my blog posts in 2013, I showed the equipment and office set-up I use for my business. In the beginning, you should start small and cheap. As you are profitable, you will want to set up systems and processes that make your business more efficient (and less back-breaking!).

The Amazing Pocket Chair® is a helpful addition to my gear for book sales. I nearly ruined my knees at one book sale, digging around in the boxes underneath the tables. Never again! This chair is small, portable and just the right height for scanning through boxes on the floor. It comes in a small bag with a handle that I can hang on my dolly. I got mine for $6 at BigLots; they're also sold on Amazon. See my supplies page on my blog for a picture and link.

Repricing Software – Although I don't talk about it much in this book, a repricing solution is critical once your inventory gets too large to handle manually. I tried several options and didn't like them because I could not get them to price exactly to my criteria. ScanPower came out with its ScanPower Repricer and I like it much better. It takes into account the other FBA offers and is tailored to FBA sellers, whereas other programs are focused on merchant sellers. ScanPower Repricer comes free with ScanPower List.

ScanPower List and ScanPower Mobile can be bought separately for $39.95 each or subscribed to as a bundle for $59.95 (with ScanPower Repricer).

MORE ON PRICING: BUY LOW, SELL HIGH

In the earlier discussion of fees, I shared with you my minimum starting point for pricing, for several types of items. Before you branch into a different category, I encourage you to run some numbers yourself so you'll be sure to know the "floor" for your prices. Your expenses may be different from mine, which may affect your floor. Amazon has raised its fees in February of each year, so you also need to make sure you are using the latest fees in your calculations.

Some categories, like toys, are also difficult to price because the product sizes, weights, shipping costs and prices vary so wildly. In addition, you never know when Amazon or another FBA seller will start a price war and slash prices. That's why I have a rule of thumb for pricing new merchandise that Chris Green taught me – 3X. Whatever the cost of the toy/appliance/electronic item, if I'm able to sell it for at least three times the cost, I'll probably be OK. At the very least, I examine it closely on my scanner and consider buying it.

I find it works best for lower priced items (under $20). For higher cost items, I may be able to make my margin with less than 3X. This is because Amazon has fixed and variable fees. With more expensive items, the fixed fees are a smaller portion of the overall price of the item and I can, thus, often charge less and get my margin. Regardless, I always look closely at the numbers once I realize that I may have a winner on my hands. The rule of thumb allows me to scan faster and discard bad deals faster so I can get to the good deals faster.

Last Christmas, several of us were selling "Dippin' Dots" toys for $65 and up. After Christmas, the price quickly dropped to around $30. Because I had bought mine for around $24, I wasn't worried about clearing out my final units – and they're selling again, for $78 this time around.

For a long time I bought potty training seats for $8 and sold them for $24.95, making $10.71 in profit – Wow! Wow because who would pay $24.95 for a plastic toilet seat? And wow because I turned an $8 investment into 133% return in two weeks. (Those seats sold like crazy.) I'd like to see the stock market achieve that kind of return on investment.

This brings me to the next very important consideration when deciding what to buy – speed of the sale, otherwise known as ranking.

BUY HIGH-TURNOVER ITEMS

Even though Amazon's warehousing fees are cheap, you don't want your inventory to sit around – you only make money when something sells. So how do you know how fast something will sell? Rank.

Amazon has millions of items in its warehouses at any given time. The faster and more recently an item has sold, the lower it will be on the rank scale. Amazon calls it velocity. Number one on the rank scale is selling the most units per minute; number 10,000,000 may not have sold a single item in years. However, it is important to note that ranking is only a snapshot in time and not indicative of future sales. If a book ranked 10,000,000 were to sell today, its ranking might drop down to 500,000 tomorrow because a sale was made the day before. I have author friends who find this very puzzling. One minute the book they wrote is ranked in the millions, and the next day it is ranked around 80,000 or less. All that indicates is that sales were made recently, which dropped the ranking. If no further sales are made, the ranking will quickly climb back up.

Amazon does not share its secret formulas, algorithms or sales data, so you have to make a best guess. I use rank to indicate that an item will sell. I've sold books with ranks over 2 million, but they took a long time to sell. Generally, I won't buy a book or media item that is ranked over 1 million unless the potential payoff is worth the potential warehouse fees. Because I had so little money to invest in inventory last year, I could not wait for a big payoff.

Another thing I've learned about this business is that I have no idea what is popular. That's why it is so crucial to scan everything and not guess. Right now I'm selling specialty plastic bags that are selling like hotcakes. I would have never thought that plastic bags would be so popular.

Earlier, we talked about fees and pricing, which are important for decision-making. Now we add in rank. If an item is ranked high, it will probably take a long time to sell; at minimum, you know it has been a while since one was sold. Although Amazon's storage fees are amazingly cheap, I'm not making any money if I'm not selling. So what is a good rank on Amazon?

I'm sorry to say, Amazon won't tell you. All Amazon has said in the past is that in books, items that are 100,000 and under will generally sell within a month (and often many copies within a month), and items that are between 100,000 and 1,000,000 will often sell within three months. I try to buy books ranked under 1,000,000 for this reason. Sometimes I will make exceptions if the return on investment is worth it. For example, I had two phonics reading programs that I bought new at BigLots for $20 each and sold for $165 each. The first one took about six weeks to sell; the second one took an additional three months. It was worth the wait to me; in fact, I wish I could find more. I was also the only FBA seller.

I've listed my buying criteria in the chart below. Let me stress here that it is my criteria, and I do not have all the answers. As you get into the business, you will conduct your own experiments and find the range with which you are most comfortable. Other FBA sellers may also tell you their criteria. I had a guest post on this topic in 2013 where Peter Valley shared his approach to rank.

In the beginning, when you are focused on fast cash, stay toward the low-ranked items and don't invest in long-term payoffs – no matter how tempting – until you can afford it. My exceptions column is where I personally might buy if the payoff was exceptional – $30 return for a 25-cent book, for example. This has changed over time for me as I made more money and could afford to wait a little bit. You'll have your own exceptions column. I'm still learning about some categories and cannot tell you what the best range is – only where I know I've made sales.

See my chart on the next page.

	Ideal rank	Upper limit	Exceptions
Books, Audio Books, Calendars	1-100,000	1,000,000	2,000,000
Textbooks	1-500,000	1,500,000	
VHS/DVDs	1-1,000	50,000	200,000
CDs	1-10,000	?	
Software	1-1,000	28,000 so far	
Video games	1-200	?	
Toys	1-75,000	165,000	360,000
Baby	1-30,000	75,000	
Health & Beauty	1-80,000	?	
Grocery	1-80,000	?	
Pets	1-80,000	?	
Home Improvement	1-20,000	?	

Electronics	Amazon does not provide rankings for some electronics; I don't know why. Where it does, I keep it below 50,000

One caveat with textbooks is that they are seasonal. They generally sell briskly in late August/September, January and June. If you are scanning in March and the textbook is ranked 1,000,000, it is worth a look – especially if the condition is Very Good – because its rank will go down during the peak selling seasons. Obviously the lower the rank the better, but I've sold textbooks for over $100 that were above 1,000,000 in rank. The higher the rank, the higher the reward I want to see.

VHS videotapes are niche products, so I don't buy them if the ranking is above 5,000 unless the video is very specialized and not available in other formats. For example, I bought a rare 1991 video of Cyrano de Bergerac for 25 cents and sold it for $25. Its ranking was 218,714. I sent it to Amazon in mid-October 2010 and it sold on May 9, 2011 – about six months. Not bad for a 25-cent investment.

With DVDs, I've not found the upper limit yet. So far, I find plenty of merchandise within these ranges and there's been nothing of such great value at a high rank that I'll risk it sitting at the warehouse for months to a year.

I've not sold a lot of software above 15,000 in rank. Often software that I buy is listed for sale in Toys & Games rather than Software, because it is a learning game for youngsters. I sold a *Top Chef* game that ranked around 16,000 in software. I sent it in March and it sold at the end of August – just over five months.

Like calendars, DVDs/games/videos don't always appear where you might think on Amazon.com. Once a product is listed on Amazon, you are generally stuck with that category. The category is usually chosen by the person who listed the item. For this reason, it is important to look at the category when you are scanning. You will NOT be able to list the product in a different category and 100,000 in Toys is different than 100,000 in Software.

I've recently found a source of cheap used video games (10 cents) and I'm experimenting with them right now.

Toys sell year round, but go crazy during the holidays. Even higher-ranked items (around 100,000) will sell quickly during this time and, in addition, selling prices are often higher. I've sold many Wii Sureshot Rifles since December 2010, starting at $30. They still rank in the low hundreds. I sold one in October 2011 at $19.50, just to give you an idea. As long as I can get them cheaply enough, I don't mind – but I'm really looking forward to the holidays again.

For baby items, I'm still experimenting to get an upper range. Generally, I buy things under 30,000 in rank. I avoid items that might be subject to a recall like car seats, strollers, cribs, etc. This is just my philosophy – I don't want the hassle should that happen. I've sold everything from baby wipes to bottles, pacifiers and spoons, to diaper bags, potty seats and booster seats. And, of course, lots of baby toys. Sometimes they are listed for sale in Amazon's baby department, and sometimes in toys – be sure to check before buying.

Ironically, many things I've bought in Pets ended up appearing in the Kitchen & Dining category. I've sold pet toys in this category that have ranked around 100,000; they took around three months to sell.

Some wall stickers I bought sold in Home Improvement. I sent them to Amazon in June; the slowest-selling one ranked just over 5,000 and took two months to sell, while the others—one ranked over 19,000—sold in June and July. That just goes to show that you can't predict customer behavior precisely with rank.

The best sources of ranking advice are other FBA sellers. One of the resources listed in the back of this book is the FBA Forum Yahoo! group [http://bit.ly/fbayahoogroup], a group committed to helping other FBA sellers be successful. I've learned a lot from them.

Go Where Others Are Not

When I walk into a store like BigLots, I know I am the only scout there. I focus on low-hanging fruit and the categories that usually give me the highest rewards. When I go to the Members-only night of a big book sale, I look around and go to where the other scanners are not. The fiction tables are usually crowded, while the textbook and non-fiction tables are usually not. At one sale, I went to the VHS tapes first and got some great bargains in Like New condition. VHS tapes are nearly always 25 cents at book sales and thrift stores, or even 10 for a $1, so there is good potential there if you can find rare videos. I want to avoid fighting for inventory, and I want to find inventory where there are not a lot of other FBA sellers.

My best returns on investment are where I am the only FBA seller, or I am one of maybe two or three, tops. In 2012, I sold a foam booster seat on Amazon for $45 where I was not only the sole FBA seller; I was the only seller, period. I sold at least one a day when I had inventory. Eventually I was discovered – there were four FBA sellers with my booster seats one day. I still sold mine for around $45, but the prices started to drop as the others competed. Competition is why I'm always looking for my next great deal.

To do this, I need to shop where the others are not. While I love BigLots – and have many categories for which I still need to scan – I know many other FBA sellers buy there too. Thus, I've branched out. I try to keep my scanner with me at all times.

One day at the Blockbuster video store. I saw a couple of tables of items that were completely unrelated to videos, like an As Seen on TV! vacuum cleaner, some toys, books, wall stickers...it was a wild mix. Everything was at least 75% off and some items were $1. I ended up buying most of the inventory and then going to other Blockbuster Video stores in my area for more. I sold the $1 wall stickers for $15, the $3 stuffed Star Wars toys for $21, the $10 vacuums for $40 and much, much more. I was usually the only FBA seller for these items and most of my inventory sold out in less than two weeks, with the rest selling over the next two months. The wall stickers were an experiment – I had never sold in the home décor category and had no idea what was a good ranking.

Chris Anderson wrote a book called *The Long Tail*, which explains that there is a buyer for almost everything and that platforms like Amazon offer an efficient way for people to reach their audiences, no matter how small. The niche culture, as he calls it, is a growing worldwide phenomenon. This is why I picked up Cyrano de Bergerac and other unusual items even though I knew they were not fast sellers. You will run across items like this as well and may decide to take a chance.

My friend Lesley has had success with some very old books that didn't even have ISBN#s (pre-1972), but that sold well once she was able to find Amazon's ID number on Amazon.com. One exciting find cost her a dollar and is so valuable that she's going to broker the sale through a rare book dealer. Although you won't find a book worth $1,500 at most book sales, you can.

I am constantly testing. Nearly every shopping trip will include some kind of experiment; whether it is the Milk-Bone brand dog toys, the adult diapers, the closet organization tool...you get the idea. The only way I'm going to learn about different categories is by testing. I don't have a lot of money, so I start small. With toys, I was lucky because Chris Green took me on a shopping trip with him to BigLots and I learned a lot. I was able to participate in the holiday season with confidence.

My goal with this book is to give you the confidence he gave me so you know what a good deal looks like and can make decisions that are profitable for you.

BE A JOINER

BigLots, Toys "R" Us, Home Depot, Sears, Kmart, JCPenney and many other retailers have customer loyalty programs that you'll want to join. They are free and give you several advantages:

* Advance notice of sales
* Special discounts and offers
* The ability to earn even greater rewards
* Online-only offers

BigLots, for example, has a special toy sale in December with huge discounts for Buzz Club reward members; members get to shop the deals several days before the public does. In addition to the discounts, BigLots gives its loyalty members coupons good for 20% off everything after 10 qualifying sales. Chris and I attacked 2010's sale, and had about six baskets of toys between us. My only regret was that I had such a limited inventory budget and therefore couldn't buy as much as I wanted.

Toys "R" Us, Wal-Mart and Target have sales, coupons and online-only deals. You can also order in quantity online if you find something hot. Sometimes they offer free shipping for orders over a certain amount, or on certain days (like Cyber Monday).

I've not yet joined Home Depot or Lowe's loyalty programs simply because I have all I can handle right now without getting into another category. A colleague of mine sells tools, which is how I learned about their programs.

Sam's Club and Costco charge an annual membership fee, but there are good deals to be found there – particularly if you can afford to buy in quantity. Chris Green told me about a product that he bought at Sam's for nearly $1,000 that he was able to turn in about a week for $2,000. He became the Club's number one buyer of that product and they ordered just for him. I don't have that kind of financial muscle right now where I can invest thousands in inventory every month – but someday I will.

Joining Tuesday Morning's program extends the time you have to return an item – very helpful if you want to return slow-moving inventory.

TAKE ACTION!

1. Review Amazon's FBA program and Prime Membership on the website until you understand how both work.
2. Become an Amazon Prime member if you are not already (or plan to become one when you can afford the annual fee).
3. Determine your inventory on hand to get started. Do you have books? CDs? DVDs? VHS tapes? Collectible/discontinued Games?
4. Are you already a member of Sam's Club or Costco? Get on their mail and email lists.
5. Join email lists for Toys "R" Us, BigLots, JCPenney, Kmart, Sears, Home Depot, Lowe's and others so you can get their online sales flyer.

4

7-Step Business Starter Checklist

This chapter is for my friend Lynn who said, "Just tell me what I need to do right now – 1, 2, 3, 4." This plan of action assumes that you will start with new and used items around your house. According to studies, the average household has over $5,000 of sellable, no longer needed new and used items, so it's a good place to start. Check off items listed below as you complete them. I have more details on these checklist items throughout the book.

1. **Plan**
   - Decide how much money you can spend on supplies and inventory to start.
   - Determine how much you need to make in order for this to be worthwhile.
   - Decide the name of your business.
   - Will you incorporate or just use a DBA to start? (DBA=Doing Business As).
   - You do not need to decide now if you want to incorporate, but make a note to yourself to think about it later. You may want to

read the *Start Your Own Corporation: Why the Rich Own Their Own Companies and Everyone Else Works for Them (Rich Dad Advisors)* book listed in the Resources chapter.

2. **Set up your business**

   - Get your desired DBA from your state. Texas has an online database you can search to be sure the business name you want is available; then you pay a small fee to own it for 10 years.

   - Go online to www.irs.gov and request a business tax ID number in the name of your DBA or corporation. Your business does not have to be incorporated to get this number. You can even get one in your name although this is not recommended.

   - File for your state sales tax number (you can do it online in most states) so you can buy merchandise tax-free. You can wait to do this until later if you want.

   - Open a separate checking account for your business. It does not have to be a business checking account per se but needs to be separate from your personal account(s) for tax purposes and for ease of accounting. Many banks (like Chase), allow you to set up accounts online.

- Sign up for a UPS business account online using your DBA. Go to http://www.ups.com and click on New User to get started.
- Review Amazon's latest fees and set up a spreadsheet to help you determine your break-even point and minimum selling prices.

3. **Order supplies.** Depending on your beginning resources, order/source these supplies. The first four are critical to start. See the Supplies page on my blog and the Resources section at the end of this book for specifics on where to get these items.

- USB handheld scanner that plugs into a USB port on your computer.
- Shipping boxes (18"x12"x12" or smaller work well for books). They don't have to be new, but they must be sturdy.
- Packing tape and paper (or bubble wrap or air pillows – NO foam peanuts).
- Free UPS shipping labels (two per 8.5"x11" page). You need to sign up and then wait about 3-4 days until you can place your first order. In the short term you can use regular paper in your printer for your boxes, but you'll like the shipping labels a lot better.

- Dymo LabelWriter 450 Turbo printer (or a Zebra printer). If you already have a printer capable of printing rolls of adhesive labels up to 2"x3" in size, that is worth testing with ScanPower or your chosen inventory listing program. Dymo and Zebra are the two that I know work for sure. For the short-term, Amazon will print off labels for you on those sheets of labels (Avery 5160) you put in your laser printer.
- Address-sized labels for your Dymo printer (they can range from 1"x2" to 2"x3" in size). I buy Dymo Compatible rather than Dymo brand. They are cheaper.
- Smartphone (ScanPower Mobile runs on phones with the Android operating system and Apple iPhone phones). Amazon.com sells cell phones as low as one penny with a two-year contract. Some month-by-month pre-paid plans and phones are inexpensive and don't require a long-term contract. For a while, Virgin was offering terrific prices on Android monthly subscription fees – around $40 a month – so be sure to shop around if you need a smartphone.
- Scanfob Bluetooth™ scanner to use with your smartphone. You don't need this to get started, but it will speed up your scouting for inventory by a lot.

- Protective carrier for your Smartphone. (I use an armband/wristband).
- Shipping scale that calculates weights up to at least 75 lbs. I started with my bathroom scale, but a real shipping scale is a lot easier to use.
- Back-up battery for your smartphone and Scanfob. See the RAVPower Element I suggest on my website.

4. **Round up your inventory from around the house**
   - Books
   - DVDs
   - CDs
   - Video games
   - VHS tapes
   - Software with packaging in good shape
   - Anything new, still sealed in its original packaging
   - Old games with all their pieces (you can sell collectible/discontinued toys on Amazon – but not used. You'd be surprised at how many games you play are discontinued.)
   - Like-New appliances or household gadgets still in their original box.

5. **Set up your Amazon seller account and ScanPower List (or whichever listing program you've chosen).**

- See   http://www.makethousandsupdates.com
  for most current links and instructions.
- Scan, price and label your items.
- Use the Finish Shipment button to send
  your items from ScanPower to Amazon
  Seller Central™.

6. **Send in your first shipment**
   - Use Amazon's Seller Central and 7-step
     Shipping Queue shipment process to
     prepare your boxes.
   - Pack and weigh your box(es).
   - Take your box(es) to a UPS drop site or
     arrange a pick-up.

7. **Go shopping for more inventory**
   - Set up your Scanfob and Smartphone.
   - Determine the locations of your local
     BigLots, Toys "R" Us, Dollar General,
     TJMaxx, Marshall's, Tuesday Morning,
     Target, Wal-Mart (and so on), thrift stores,
     and library branches. See Chapters 13 and
     14 for ideas of where to find inventory.
   - Find out about local book sales by calling
     your library branches or looking at their
     Friends of the Public Library sites online,
     checking out newspapers and looking at
     sites like these: Book Sale Finder:
     www.booksalefinder.com, Book Sale

Manager: www.booksalemanager.com.
Book   Sales   Found:
http://bit.ly/FREEtrialFrank.

* Look for garage and estate sales.
* Note all local church/temple rummage sales in your calendar as they occur throughout the year – they'll occur about the same time again next year.

5

WHAT CAN I SELL ON AMAZON?

You can sell just about anything with a barcode on Amazon – toys, games, home goods, bedding, books, computers, software, electronics, pet supplies, tools, food, appliances and much, much more. There are several categories of restricted goods. Some of them (like clothing and automotive) require permission from Amazon first and others (like guns) simply cannot be sold on the site. Some categories, like toys and games, are NOT restricted if you are an FBA seller, but are restricted during the holiday season if you are a merchant seller. This is because Amazon handles the fulfillment and controls the customer experience; Amazon is obsessed with providing a good experience for its customers. Being able to sell toys at Christmas without restriction is another big benefit to being an FBA seller.

Restricted items:
- Hazardous materials
- Certain batteries
- Certain liquids
- Live animals
- Items that weigh more than 150 lbs.

* Many pornographic materials
* Jewelry
* Clothing

You can sell in these categories immediately:
* Baby
* Books*
* Beauty
* Camera & Photo
* DVDs*
* Electronics
* Everything Else
* Grocery
* Health & Personal Care
* Home & Garden
* Music*
* Musical Instruments
* Office Products
* Software
* Sports & Outdoors
* Tools & Home Improvement
* Toys & Games
* Video Games
* Videos*

* You will only be able to list these products to the extent that Amazon makes available functionality to list such products. In other words, you can sell books but not magazines, CDs but not MP3 files — that kind of thing.

There are several places where you can find all these rules and exceptions: 1) your contract. Print it off and read it more than once; 2) on Seller Central in Amazon (look under Help) and; 3) in the FBA Manual also found in Seller Central. You'll want to refer to this a lot in the beginning.

You can submit a request to Amazon to sell in these categories. Read the rules first. Many simply require you to have been a seller with Amazon for a certain amount of time. Others – like Collectible Books – require a special knowledge or expertise in the category in order to sell:

* Clothing & Accessories
* Automotive Parts, Motorcycle & ATV
* Cell Phones & Accessories
* Collectible Books
* Jewelry
* Personal Computers
* Shoes
* Watches

This list is by no means comprehensive. You can find a complete list through your Amazon Seller Central account [look under the FBA Manual under Help. Be sure to check the list if you are entering a new category as the rules might have changed since the last time you looked. For example, Amazon now allows its FBA Sellers to sell non-media overseas, so I expect there will be even more rule changes.

Currently you can sell all your media on overseas Amazon sites. This includes books, DVDs, videos, CDs, video games and software. Once your seller account is established it is very easy to arrange to sell media internationally. Under the Inventory tab in Seller Central, go to the Inventory Amazon Fulfills page. There is a button to click to sell internationally. You will be required to send in a PDF of your signature for their records and that's it! Now your media listings will be visible on several international sites.

My books are better traveled than I am. I sold a book to someone in Sofia, Bulgaria once.

One caveat to keep in mind is that with the exception of media, Amazon insists that most items for sale be new or, possibly Collectible as in the case of discontinued toys and games. Some categories allow Open Box items which are basically new but the box has been opened. Remember that donut maker you got for Christmas and only used once? Now's your chance to make room in your cabinets and get rid of it. For used clothing, etc., you'll want to use eBay. Amazon has also returned items to me that were damaged in the warehouse; I was then able to sell these items on eBay or Craigslist with a picture and an explanation that it was brand new with a slightly damaged box.

TAKE ACTION!

1. Read all the categories on Amazon's website.
2. Spend time looking at the top sellers in each category to get a feel for them.
3. Determine which categories are most appealing to you and make sure you understand any requirements or restrictions. The Help section of Seller Central will have a complete list.

4. For your chosen categories, create a spreadsheet of your own to help you understand your margins and minimum pricing. If you are selling something heavy, like tools or cans of food, be sure to adjust for the extra shipping costs.

6

IS IT HARD TO FIND INVENTORY?

Finding inventory is the easiest part of this business. There is more potential inventory than I can possibly buy with my budget. Almost everywhere I turn, there are opportunities. For this reason, it is very important to have a specific budget and criteria in mind when shopping, or else you can spend like crazy.

Thrift stores – There are hundreds of thrift stores in my area. I've barely explored them because the ones I've visited have been so good that I run out of money before I run out of opportunities. Generally, I find books, videos, CDs, audio books, collectible toys and – sometimes – new toys still sealed in their boxes. Often there are special sales dates that are worth noting. For example, one thrift store I mentioned earlier offers 20-cent hardbacks and 10-cent paperbacks on Saturdays between 10 a.m. and 2 p.m. I wrote a blog post on how I shop Goodwill stores that you can find on my members-only site.

Book sales – Spring and fall are the biggest seasons for book sales. There are several kinds: library book sales, school district book sales, warehouse sales/auctions, retail book sales and other book sales. Usually a book sale is to support a group or charity. Big sales will often be listed on book sale websites like

www.booksalefinder.com   or
www.booksalemanager.com.

In addition, libraries have societies called Friends of the Library that usually host the twice annually book sale(s). These sales can be at the branch level or for a whole library system. We have both types of sales in the Dallas-Fort Worth Metroplex where I live. Arlington, for example, has one big library sale twice a year for all its branches, while Dallas lets each branch host its own. If you can't find information on the library branch website, call them.

Prices at these sales tend to be 25 cents for videos, $1-$2 for DVDs and CDs, 50 cents to $1 for paperbacks and $1-$2 for hardbacks. Often there is a small fee to become a friend of the library, which is well worth it because it gives you advance notice of the sales and early entry into the sale. Universities sometimes have book sales as do charitable groups like the local ASPCA.

Warehouse sales and auctions are often announced in the newspaper and are for large lots of books. These books may have been acquired as lost property (think of the postal service or the airport) when the owner could not be found or may be from a retail store looking to get rid of poor-performing merchandise or perhaps going out of business like Borders did in 2011. Sometimes a large library book sale will sell off the remainders to the highest bidder at the end of the sale. I bought approximately 30,000 books from a library book sale with two friends of mine. We feel a bit like the dog that caught the car as we are still sorting through and packing them up to sell over a year later.

Retail stores will often have ongoing sale tables in addition to big sales a few times a year. In North Texas, we have Half Price Books, which has fabulous sales with discounts off their already low prices. In November 2011, they had a warehouse sale for the first time and everything was $3 or less. Barnes & Noble regularly has discount sections and sale tables. Stores like Wal-Mart, Sam's Club, Target and others also sell books and media — just keep an eye out for clearance items. BigLots has books from 25 cents and up. It's a mixed bag there — I've learned the hard way that a lot of other FBA sellers shop at BigLots, and sometimes it takes me months to clear multiples of books bought there. Basically, if a book ends up at BigLots, it is because no one wanted it in the mainstream stores.

At my local Blockbuster Video, I bought a few books that shouldn't have been there in the first place. They were brand new and sold nicely online. The lesson to me was to look around everywhere I go and to bring my scanner.

To find out about sales, I get on as many mail/email lists as possible. It means setting up folders in my Outlook email box to handle the deluge of email, but it is worth it. If you go to a book sale, be sure to get on their mailing list for next time (usually by becoming a Friend, but not always).

Ongoing library book sales are slightly different from other book sales in that they are going on all the time. The library generally has a room or alcove where there are books for sale and you can go any time to shop. New books come in as donations are made or as the library clears its shelves. In Dallas, the downtown public library has a permanent bookstore inside the library. In addition to the prices listed daily, once a month they sell books for $5 a box (bring your own box). Fort Worth has a similar arrangement. In addition to the ongoing sale, the Fort Worth library also has big annual sales, with even more heavily discounted prices, that it advertises to the public. You can find out about these ongoing sales either at the book sale finder websites (see Resources at the end of the book), on your library's website, or by calling the main branches of the libraries in your area.

Discount stores like BigLots tend to get books in huge lots that are basically overstocks. Scan with care to make sure you are not competing with a bunch of other FBA sellers. Other discount stores like Dollar Tree and the Dollar Store have yielded finds. The great thing about buying at a retail store is that the book/video game/CD/DVD is new and more likely to get you a higher price. Wal-Mart, Sam's, Costco and others will quickly clear out a book or media item that is not selling fast enough for their business model. These media items are often still quite popular and can be good sellers for you.

Discount stores are also a great source of new toys, games and other merchandise to sell on Amazon. I've shopped Marshall's, TJ Maxx, Tuesday Morning, Target, Wal-Mart, Kmart and a few specialty shops over the past year with good results.

Other Amazon sellers sometimes sell books for ridiculously low prices. Often these mistakes come from not understanding how to use their repricer. If you see a hot book (possibly because you want to sell it yourself) selling for one penny or even $1 FBA, it may make sense to buy it and then re-sell it. Someone is going to buy that book, and might as well be you. (This strategy assumes you are a Prime member and will get free shipping on the item.) Most sellers only need to make a mistake like that once or twice before they fix the problem with their inventory repricer.

Other sources of inventory include estate sales, storage unit auctions and many more. Although I've not yet ventured into all of these areas, there is a good book on this topic listed in the Resources section. If you are like me, you'll have more opportunities than money in the beginning so you won't need to branch out until your business is bigger. I have several blog posts about inventory that I've posted on my members site for you.

TAKE ACTION!

1. Go to Google Maps and search for BigLots, Wal-Mart, Target, etc. to find out which retailers and discount stores are near you.
2. Do another search for thrift stores in a five-mile radius. Create a driving map for yourself so you can check them out efficiently when you are ready. Increase your radius as needed until you have at least five stores to explore.
3. Check out www.booksalefinder.com, Book Sales Found, and www.booksalemanager.com to find book sales in your area. Also, start keeping a calendar of books sales as you find them — many sales are not on these lists.
4. Find the nearest library to you as well as the city's main branch, determine how they run their book sales and when the next one(s) will be. Do the same for other nearby cities.

7

Does It Take A Lot Of Time?

On average, I spend about 10 hours a week on my Amazon business. In reality, it is more like 40 hours a month spent in big bursts. I may go to a big book sale or on a shopping trip and then spend a few more hours boxing things up and sending to Amazon. Afterward, I might do nothing for a couple of weeks aside from some repricing. The flexibility of this business is one of its more appealing facets. Here's my hours breakout:

* One-time up-front learning and set-up: about 15-20 hours, depending on your level of comfort with technology and how much reading you want to do in advance
    o Amazon Seller set-up
    o FBA set-up
    o Listing and scouting tools
    o Books to read (see resources)
* Supply acquisition: 1 hour every few months to drive to Uline (a store that stocks packing and mailing supplies) for more boxes or tape.
* Inventory acquisition: 3-4 hours a week depending on my schedule.

- Preparing shipments to Amazon: 5-6 hours a week, depending on number of boxes.
- Re-pricing: 1-2 hours as needed, about once or twice a month.
- Tax/bookkeeping: ongoing, a few hours a month.

I already have a business that I own so my time to set up the business legally and with a tax ID was zero. I am using a DBA (doing business as) and C corporation that I already own, so I'm running the Amazon business and its accounting through my current corporate entity.

If you are not incorporated yet, I suggest you look into it for legal and tax reasons that are quite profitable. If you incorporate, you can pay your taxes like a corporation (i.e., <u>after</u> all expenses have been paid) instead of as an individual (<u>before</u> paying for expenses) which can save you a lot of money.

If you at least have a DBA, you will be able to get a sales tax certificate, which in Texas saves me 8.25% on purchases. You will also be able to open up a business bank account, which I highly recommend.

Since my business was already incorporated in Texas and I have other businesses here, I didn't pursue other options. If this is your only business, you may want to consider incorporating in Nevada. It is an excellent state for online resellers for several reasons:

1. Extreme privacy laws provide better protection for you as a business owner.
2. Inexpensive incorporation and PO Box services available to keep you legally a Nevada corporation.
3. You can write off your trips to Las Vegas (just kidding...maybe. It depends on the business portion of your trip).

Just so you know, your business does not need to be in the same state in which you live if it is a business that sells nationwide. There are several good resources to consult regarding incorporation, including *Start Your Own Corporation: Why the Rich Own Their Own Companies and Everyone Else Works for Them* (http://bit.ly/GarrettSuttonIncBook) and Inc. and Grow Rich (http://amzn.to/incandgrow), both of which have helped me enormously over the past 17 years.

If you look at my sales numbers for last year, you'll see that there were months during which I barely worked my Amazon business and others during which I worked a lot more than 40 hours a month. Your business will do better the more time you can give it, of course, but the real question to ask yourself is whether it will perform well enough in the time you have to give.

TAKE ACTION!

1. Secure any DBA(s) you want to use with your business.
2. You can get a DBA even if you are not incorporated. Because incorporation can take a few weeks, go ahead and get your DBA first and use it to register with Amazon and to set up a bank account. In many states you can search DBAs online to determine if the one you want is already taken – much like going to "Go Daddy" to see if a URL is available. Then you can register in person or mail in the paperwork to secure your DBA.

3. Open a bank account for business use only.
4. Get your sales tax certificate from the state in which you are incorporated. In Texas, most of the paperwork can be done online.
5. Consider incorporating. Research the advantages/disadvantages of incorporating.

8

What Do I Need To Make It Work?

I wrote this chapter for the reader who skipped to this question. You sequential readers will find parts of it repetitive.

You can start this business very modestly and work your way up. Here are the tools I use to run my business today. I note which ones are necessary from the beginning and which can be added later as you have more money.

To list on Amazon:

- **Handheld USB scanner** – almost any kind will do. Amazon sells several for under $30. They plug into a USB port on your computer and allow you to scan ISBN and UPC codes into your computer. You can type in the codes manually, but using a scanner is much faster and easier.

- **ScanPower** – www.scanpower.com. The first two weeks are free. Click on https://unity.scanpower.com/register. For those who bought my eBook follow the instructions in the email I sent you to get an additional two weeks free for a total of a month. After that, it is $39.95 a month.

- If you don't like ScanPower after trying it, or simply wish to look at more options for listing and mobile tools for FBA sellers, I've listed contact information and details on the other providers on my members site. I write about ScanPower because I know it, but it does not matter to me what program you use. The important thing is to have a program that allows you to easily and efficiently list your inventory and scout from your smartphone.

To ship to Amazon:
- **LabelWriter Turbo 450 or Zebra label printer** – To print labels as you go. Because Amazon will print labels for you for free, on 8.5"x11" sheets (30 to a page – Avery 5160 labels), you can wait on this if need be.
- **Labels** – No need to buy brand name labels; get the cheapest you can that are address size. My labels cost me less than half a penny each. Dymo Compatible is cheaper than Dymo.
- **Packing tape** – I recommend 3" tape so you can cover all seams in one swipe. Uline (www.uline.com) sells tape by the case and gives you a free industrial tape dispenser to go with it. Some people, particularly those with small children, prefer the silent tape, but it costs more.
- **Boxes** – Book sales will often have lots of good book boxes lying around, which will help offset your costs, but you'll still need to buy some boxes

new. I buy from Uline, which has a warehouse near me so I don't pay shipping costs. I get my book boxes (18x12x12) for 90 cents when I buy 25.

- **Packing paper or bubble wrap** – To date I've not had to buy any bubble wrap or air pillows because I had a supply in my garage. I get more as things are mailed to me. My packing paper – also called clean newsprint came on a huge roll from Uline. Amazon is particular as to what they will let you use as filler (no foam peanuts, for example), so be sure to read their shipping instructions carefully.
- **UPS account** – Free. You need it so you can get free adhesive shipping labels and arrange pick-ups of large orders. The labels you need are on 8.5"x11" paper (two labels per sheet) that feeds into your printer. You will need one sheet per box that you ship. Generally, UPS will send you 50 sheets at a time, delivered to your door for free. You can also print labels on paper in a pinch, but adhesive labels are better.

  You will also need a UPS account if you plan to have shipments picked up at your house. I do this when I have a lot of boxes, especially toy boxes that are much bigger and harder to fit in my car. It costs anywhere from $6 to $9 for a UPS pick-up, depending on fuel surcharges. This is a flat fee regardless of the number of boxes and is an excellent service for big shipments. You do NOT need a UPS account to ship to Amazon because you will be using Amazon's account. More on this later.
- **Black permanent marker pen** – Can't live without this. I use it to mark my book boxes at book sales

and to help me weigh and mark my book boxes at home.

- **Scale** – I started with my bathroom scale. Eventually you'll want a digital scale designed for packages, with a flat top. It is hard to stand on a scale with a 50-pound box and get an accurate read. I bought a WeighMax [http://amzn.to/weighmax] digital scale on Amazon for about $20. It weighs packages up to 75 lbs., which is plenty because you are not supposed to ship boxes heavier than 50 lbs. to Amazon.

To scout for inventory:
- **Scanfob** – This is the Bluetooth scanner I use for scouting. It costs approximately $400 although you can get a discount code for about $100 off from my website. Obviously if you don't have the money for it now, save up for it. In the meantime, you can scan barcodes into your smartphone using the camera on your phone or read them in using the voice entry feature. It is slower, but free. Other Bluetooth scanners are available and may be less expensive. I am not familiar with these other scanners, so make sure the scanner works with your mobile app before you buy it. I like my Scanfob because I can scan from a fair distance from the item. I am short and many interesting boxes are on top shelves so I find that feature useful. It is also very fast.
- **ScanPower Mobile**– A monthly data subscription fee of $39.95. (The application itself is free.) If you are also a ScanPower List customer, you get a bundled price of $59.95 for both services. You will want this once you start scouting in earnest. I

personally like it the best because it shows you FBA offers as well as new and used prices. It gives you the net you'll make after Amazon's fees and commissions and it also tells you how many units the other sellers have. It is a crucial tool for my business. Many newcomers have started with a product called <u>Profit Bandit</u> because it is much less expensive than ScanPower – a one-time fee of $15. I find it harder to read, and it doesn't offer all the features of ScanPower, but I think it is a good solution for someone starting on a tight budget.

- **Smartphone** – ScanPower Mobile runs on iPhone, iPad, iPod touch and phones with Android. As long as you have one of these devices, you can scout with ScanPower Mobile. I was able to get my Android phone from Amazon (yes, they sell cellular service too!) for one penny when I extended my AT&T service for an additional two years. They even delivered my phone overnight. It is one heck of a deal. I then sold my iPhone on Craigslist. This was before the iPhone version of ScanPower Mobile was available.
- **Armband/wristband** – I use this to hold and protect my phone, and free up my hands. It is about $8 at Amazon. Not critical, of course, but helpful.

<u>Other tools:</u>
- **ScanPower Repricer**– This comes with ScanPower for free. It allows you to either manually or automatically reprice your entire inventory. I usually reprice manually, but I've done both.
- **Excel** – Most Amazon reports and the repricer export data into a format that is opened by Excel

software. If you are not familiar with Excel, you will need to spend some time learning the basics of how to sort data and move data around in a spreadsheet. Other spreadsheet programs may also be able to open these files as well.

* **Un-du label remover** – A solvent for those darned sticky price labels that BigLots and other retailers put on their products. I now buy it in bulk at Uline.com, but you can find it online or at office supply stores. A little goes a long way and it works great without damaging the packaging. Other sellers swear by Goof-Off, but I found it doesn't work so well with the BigLots stickers (they are heinous).

* **Scotty Peelers** – A miracle for peeling off labels. The peelers get under the label and lift it off.

TAKE ACTION!

1. Look at this list and take note of items you may already have and items you need to get started. *At a minimum you will want a scanner, shipping labels from UPS and sheet labels (for Amazon) for your printer.*

2. This list assumes you have a computer with internet access and a printer. If you don't have these items, think about whose equipment you might be able to borrow or share until you can buy your own.

3. Is your phone a smartphone? If not, get one.

4. Do you have packing materials? If not, you may be able to get materials for free or very cheap

on Craigslist (from people moving, etc.). Just be sure the boxes are still strong enough for books and the packing paper is clean (no newspapers).

9

How Much Does It Cost To Get Started?

As I mentioned earlier in the book, I started out Spartan. I bought a USB scanner (about $30), a LabelWriter 450 Turbo with labels (about $110 in all), 25 book boxes ($25) and a crate of tape (about $50). I packed up and shipped books from my shelves. I got a free month with ScanPower and was determined to make the most of it.

I signed up with Amazon, which cost me, $39.99 a month but the first month was free. I sent boxes to Amazon, which did not cost me shipping up front.

Once I went through my inventory and made some money, I was ready to scout for new inventory. I rented ASellerTool's PDA solution off eBay because renting was cheaper than buying at the time. ASellerTool still cost me about $345 to get started but I got $285 back later when I returned the PDA. I also had a monthly subscription fee of $44.95 with ASellerTool for the data. As I said, it was the best deal around at the time. ScanPower Mobile is cheaper to get started.

When ScanPower Mobile came out late in 2010, I returned the ASellerTool hardware and used my deposit return to buy the Scanfob 2002 ($282). I started using the

Scanfob and ScanPower Mobile in December 2010 and it made a huge difference in my business. Along the way, as I made money I put some back into inventory, some toward my family and some toward things like the digital scale, more boxes, more labels, etc.

So, to answer the question of how much does it cost to get started – as little as $200 and as much as $640 plus inventory and shipping costs:

Item	Cost
USB Scanner	$30
LabelWriter 450 Turbo	$90
Labels	$20
Boxes	$25
Tape	$50
ScanPower (first month free)	$39.95 ($59.95 bundle with ScanPower Mobile)/month
ScanPower Mobile	$39.95/month or bundle
Digital Scale	$22.50
Scanfob	$282
Smartphone	$.01 (with a 2-year commitment)
Un-du	$8-$10
Armband/wristband smartphone holder	$10-$12
Amazon Pro Seller account	$39.99/month[6]
Shipping	25-50 cents a pound, roughly

---

[6]The first month is free so if you work hard the first month, you can earn enough in sales to offset your costs.

TAKE ACTION!

1. Determine your starting budget.
2. Order/pick up your supplies.
3. See if there is a Uline warehouse near you. If not, you will probably need to source your boxes, tape, etc. somewhere else because shipping from Uline can be high. Look for a wholesaler/warehouse in your area. It may be advantageous to take a trip to Atlanta, Chicago, Dallas, etc., to get supplies a few times a year. Also, check out Wal-Mart and Sam's Club. Some sellers have found good prices on boxes there.
4. If you want to start small, your local office supply superstore should have what you need as well – it will cost more per unit, but you can get a roll of tape for $4 rather than $50 for a case.

10

Ready? Set...

Don't read this chapter until you are in front of your computer and ready to set up your Amazon Pro Seller account and ScanPower. This is very hands-on.

Please note that changes at ScanPower or Amazon may have affected these directions. I suggest you check my updates at http://www.makethousandsupdates.com if you get stuck or something doesn't look right to make sure you are following the most current directions. Because technology changes so quickly, I learned it is hard to keep this book current. The update page will have the most current links and directions. What I will focus on in this chapter is the *process* and where to go to get detailed directions.

If you are using another listing product, then just set up your Amazon Pro Seller account and look at the rest of the chapter for the process. Other listing programs and scouting programs will have a similar process to get set up. Most likely they will have instructions, videos, etc., to help you get started.

OK, now to get started! ScanPower has an excellent step-by-step on its website on how to set up your Amazon Pro Seller account and connect ScanPower to it: http://www.scanpower.com/step-1/. Again, if this link isn't working or has changed, check my updates. If you get stuck at any point in setting up your ScanPower List and/or Mobile programs, don't hesitate to contact them at: support@scanpower.com. They are quick to email you back with help.

STEP ONE: GET A PRO SELLER ACCOUNT

To sell on Amazon, you need a seller account. This is different from your customer account that you probably already have. Each person/company on Amazon is allowed to have one seller account. While you can use the same email you use for your personal account, you must have a different password.

Many sellers choose to have a unique email and password for their seller accounts. This is up to you. No one will ever see your email or your password except Amazon.

Since you are only allowed one seller account, I suggest you first have your "doing business as" or DBA name in place. You don't want to list on Amazon under your own name. You can add a logo later if you want, and you can even change your seller name in the future if you want, but it makes sense to think about it now. Amazon insists that your name be unique and not infringe on anyone else's trademark. The easiest way to do this is to secure a legal DBA through your state. It is not necessary to register your DBA nationwide. In my state, it costs $10 to get a DBA, $25 to register it statewide for 10 years which is what I did.

Most Amazon customers don't care what your name is because they are really buying from Amazon, but they may unconsciously choose your competitor over you if your name seems unprofessional.

Ready? Ok. Go to http://services.amazon.com/content/sell-on-amazon.htm. Part way down the page, click on the Start Selling button under Sell Professionally. Your first month is free, a $39.99 savings, which gives you time to get a lot of inventory up to Amazon.com if you hustle.(Please note: Amazon could change this at any time, but it has been true for three years now that the first month is free.)

In addition to your business name, you will need:

* Business address and contact information
* A credit or debit card with valid billing address
* Phone number where you can be reached
* Your tax ID information

While you are signing up, they may give you the option for an Amazon Webstore. Most people will not want or need this. It makes sense for people who are selling their own merchandise (something they design or manufacture themselves) and who want a separate website from Amazon that is integrated with Amazon. Again, very few of my readers fall into that category.

Most of us simply want to buy things to sell on Amazon.com, not run an e-commerce company. For those who want a website, I strongly suggest you talk to Amazon first about your needs before signing up.

Moving on. Before you click on Continue at the bottom of the page, take a moment to print off your Agreement. It will be a blue link next to a box you must check that says "I have read and accepted the terms and conditions of the Agreement."

You don't need to read it now, but you should read it in the future and you may need to read it many times. In addition, in your agreement near the bottom (just skim along) there is a blue link to FBA Guidelines. Go ahead and print that off as well. You will be able to access your Agreement and FBA Guidelines from the Help page of your Amazon Seller Central dashboard, but you might as well get them now rather than hunt for them later. I printed mine off and put them in a three-ring binder and I probably read them about once a year to refresh myself on some detail or another.

It has been a while since I signed up, but at some point you will also need to give Amazon your bank account information where you want your checks deposited (hooray!) and your sales tax certificate number. If you don't have one yet, don't worry about it. You can add it later.

What If I already have a seller account?

Perhaps you've sold some items on Amazon.com as a personal seller and now you're wondering if you need to go Pro. The short answer is "yes." Only Pro sellers can work with third-party software providers like the listing software guys. In addition, it is much cheaper to go Pro if you are selling more than 40 items a month. I sell hundreds of items a month. In addition, the reporting and support for Pro sellers is much greater.

You can use FBA without being Pro, but you'll want to switch pretty quickly once you have a lot of inventory up there and then it will be a real hassle. It is simpler to do it now, at the beginning. If you have listings on Amazon already and want to switch to Pro from an individual/personal seller account, I suggest you talk with Amazon.com directly.

Here are the directions to upgrade from Amazon.com's website (which I found through the Help page), but please be aware that Amazon could change this at any time:

1. *Go to the Settings link and select Account Info.*
2. *On the Seller Account Information page, scroll down to the Selling Plan section and click Modify Plan.*
3. *Click the Upgrade button.*
4. *Review the terms on the next page and then click the Proceed to Upgrade button.*

After clicking the Proceed to Upgrade button, you will be returned to your Account Info page and see a message indicating that the upgrade process has begun.

Your subscription to the Professional selling plan will begin immediately, and additional links to Professional seller tools will appear in your account. Some billing features may take up to 30 minutes to become effective.

Once the upgrade process is completed, you will no longer be charged a per-item fee. The first month's subscription fee will be debited to your seller account immediately and monthly thereafter. You can see the monthly subscription fee in the Payments pages of your seller account.

This is fine and dandy if you are happy with your seller name, but what if you want a more business-like name or a new DBA? You will have to change it on your Seller Account Information page:

To change the business information for your seller account, follow these steps:

1. *On the **Settings** link, select **Account Info**.*
2. *Click the **Edit** button next to the section that you want to update.*
3. *Enter new information or edit your current information.*
4. *Click **Submit** to save your changes.*

In addition, you might want to ask other sellers about their experience becoming Pro after selling as an individual. The FBA Forum Yahoo Group is very helpful and active. You'll get responses in less than a day: http://bit.ly/FBAForum.

Once you are set up as a Pro Seller, you can move on to the next step.

STEP TWO: CONNECT YOUR ACCOUNT TO YOUR LISTING PROGRAM

Now that you are a Pro Seller, you have the ability to interface with third-party software options like ScanPower, Listtee and others. Obviously, I'm pleased with ScanPower and have used them for years, but I don't care what you use, just that you have a program to make your business efficient and fast. If you're going to send in hundreds to thousands of items a month, you need a system – and sending in lots of high-margin inventory with fast turnover is how you make money.

If you want to look at the other programs out there before making up your mind, check out my member site. I have information on Tools that I keep updated there.

Most of them are priced right around $60 a month if you use the listing program and the scouting program.

If you are using ScanPower, you need to go to: https://unity.scanpower.com/register. There is a simple walk-through sign-up. You will be asked to give your credit card information even though you won't be charged right away. Those of you who bought my eBook need to check the email I sent in the beginning with all the links. There are simple instructions in that email for how to get your free month.

After you sign up, the program will take you through the process of connecting ScanPower to your Amazon Pro Seller account.

Be sure to remember your email and password! I used the same email and password that I use for my Amazon seller account. The reason you need to make sure to remember it is you will need it again to connect ScanPower Mobile on your smartphone to your ScanPower account on your computer. All the programs work together.

And that's it! You're in! Here are some links to helpful videos and screenshots about ScanPower. In addition, I have information on the program on my blog and in my member site:

- ScanPower's YouTube video: http://youtu.be/dzstUlE_xmY
- Attaching your ScanPower account to your Pro Seller account (click on "Step 2"): http://www.scanpower.com/support/listing-repricing/
- How to set up ScanPower List: http://www.scanpower.com/u2-list-instructions/
- A Step-by-Step Guide I created for adjusting your ScanPower List settings:

http://www.scribd.com/doc/162230737/New-ScanPower-Step-by-Step-for-Amazon-FBA-Sellers

If any of these links don't work, please check out my updates online http://www.makethousandsupdates.com. I learned with the first version of the book that webpages change much faster than book rewrites! I will do my best to keep everything up-to-date online.

Do I have to use listing software to sell on Amazon?

The short answer to this question is "no." Amazon is set up such that you can create new catalog listings and add to existing catalog items from your Seller Central Pro Seller account. I tried it and found it to be very slow and time consuming. Using a listing program like ScanPower or Listtee makes me more efficient and faster. But, if you have more time than money at this point, wait to use a listing program. The ladies over at **Thrifting for Profit** made a YouTube video that shows you how to list FBA items through Amazon Seller Central: http://youtu.be/qzZYCFarJY4.

STEP THREE: CONNECT YOUR SCOUTING TOOL

For those of you who will be processing inventory from around the house, you don't need a scouting tool right away. I didn't need one until after my first month. ScanPower Mobile not only provides all the great data of ScanPower List on the go, it also integrates with ScanPower List. What does that mean to you? It means that when you decide to buy something you are scanning at the store, you click Buy and that item will be sent to the ScanPower List program for you. When you get home, all you need to do is price the item and add any notes. It saves time not having to scan the item in again to list it.

To set up ScanPower Mobile, you need to first download the application or "app" from the appropriate smartphone store. If you are using an iPhone, that will be iTunes. If you are using an Android-based phone, that will be the Google Play store. Click on either the iTunes logo (iPhone users) or Google Play store logo (Android) on your phone. If it is not on your front screen, it will be under Applications.

The application is free. Click on Install and it will install to your phone.

Next, you need to subscribe to the monthly data plan. You may have already purchased the List/Mobile bundle as part of the set-up process for ScanPower List. If not, login to your ScanPower account: http://unity.scanpower.com.

Click on the red Settings link at the top of the page and choose Account. From here, choose Subscriptions at the top of the page. You will now be able to add on ScanPower Mobile to your account. Choose the bundle at the top of the page for $59.95.

Go to the very bottom of the page and click Save.

Now that you've signed up for ScanPower Mobile (also called Scout) and have downloaded the app to your phone, you need to connect the app to your data subscription.

ScanPower has simple instructions with pictures for you at this link: http://www.scanpower.com/support/mobile-apps/. I found this under Support and Mobile Apps so if the link changes in the future, you can look for it that way or you can check out my updates at: http://www.makethousandsupdates.com.

For iPhone users, you will need to go to your settings icon which looks like a gear and then you will need to scroll down until you find ScanPower. Once you click on the ScanPower settings, you will be able to add your email address and password.

For Android users, you can access the settings inside the ScanPower application. Open the app on your phone. Click on the permanent menu button at the bottom of your phone screen. It will usually be on the far left underneath the brand of your phone (mine is Samsung for example). That button that looks like a piece of paper is your menu button. Click on it and a menu will pop up. Choose Device Settings and enter your email and password.

Once you've added your email and password, you are connected to ScanPower's live data.

There are still two more things to do to make your ScanPower work optimally:

1. Connect your phone camera to ScanPower Mobile.
2. Connect your Bluetooth Scanner to ScanPower Mobile.

iPhone users don't need to do anything to connect their phone camera to ScanPower. Android phone users need to download another application from the Google Play store called ZXing Barcode Scanner. It is free. Type in the name at the top of the Google Play store screen and it will appear. Install it and you are set to go!

Now you can use ScanPower mobile. Go ahead and test it on a book or anything around your house that has a barcode:

1. Open ScanPower.
2. At the top of the screen on the far right you will see a button that looks like a barcode. Click it.
3. A screen with a red line pops up.
4. Center your barcode within the screen.
5. Once the phone grabs the barcode, you will be taken back to the main ScanPower screen.
6. Read the data that is pulled up.

Assuming that you now see data on your book/object, then everything is working!

If you've bought the Scanfob 2005 Bluetooth Scanner to work with your ScanPower Mobile (again, if you are using another program, the process will be similar), then you need to set that up next.

Make sure that you set up your Scanfob and phone at home before you go scouting the first time. I am often surprised at how many people go shopping without doing this first and then end up frustrated because they can't get the technology to work. Serial IO which is the company that makes the Scanfob, has great customer support, but you can't call them from the phone that you are trying to set up. You need to call them from home, get it working and then go shopping.

If you are buying your Scanfob new, you will get a Scanfob 2005. You can get a discount on it by using a coupon/code that I have on my blog.

If you are buying a used one off of eBay or another website, then you will probably be buying the Scanfob

2002. The instructions are different depending on which version you have.

ScanPower has instructions for Android and iPhone with pictures for the **Scanfob 2002** at this link: http://www.scanpower.com/support/mobile-apps/. You need to scroll down the page past the ScanPower Mobile set up instructions.

Since most of my readers will be buying their Scanfob new, I will focus on the 2005. Scanfob 2005 comes with a piece of paper that has instructions and barcodes to scan. If yours didn't for some reason or you've misplaced it, you can download another copy here:http://serialio.com/support/Scanner/Scanfob_2002/Docs/Scanfob-2005-BT-Setup-SPP-HID.pdf. When you click on that link, the document will be downloaded to your computer. Look in your Downloads folder if you cannot find it.

The first thing you need to do when you get your Scanfob is to charge it for about 4 hours. It comes with only a partial charge.

Look at your setup document. You want your Scanfob in **HID mode**. This is on the *second* page of your instructions. You do **NOT** want SPP mode. Android smartphone users no longer need SerialMagic Gears if they have the Scanfob 2005. Any instructions you see for SerialMagic Gears can be ignored unless you have an earlier version of the Scanfob.

I know this sound like gibberish, but it will make more sense when you have your instruction sheet in front of you.

Some readers have trouble with Step 4 of the instructions that say, "Make your device discoverable." If you are not familiar with Bluetooth devices, that can sound really weird. What you need to do is go to the

Bluetooth settings on your phone. On an Android phone you can find them under Applications and Settings. The Settings icon looks like a big gear. On the iPhone you are also looking for the big gear. You may need to locate Wireless and Network under the settings before you find the Bluetooth settings.

Once you've found your Bluetooth settings, you need to make sure Bluetooth is on. Usually the default setting is off. Once you turn it on, click on the Bluetooth icon to go to the more advanced settings.

You should see the name of your phone there. Mine is a SAMSUNG-SGH-I727...whatever that means. There is usually a check box that will make your phone visible to Bluetooth devices for a couple of minutes. This is what Scanfob means by "Make your device discoverable." Now you can move on to Step 5.

If your phone is an Android, you will scan the iOS & Windows barcode. If your phone is an iPhone, you will scan the Mac OSX barcode.

Lastly, if you look at the bottom of the page, you will see an option to turn the Scanfob beep off and on. I keep mine turned off so I don't draw too much attention in stores. Some people prefer to have it on because then they know the scanner grabbed the barcode.

Now go ahead and open ScanPower and scan something with your Scanfob 2005. If the data pulls up, you are all set! If you are having trouble, call the friendly guys at Serial IO for help: 512-994-3630.

Do I Have to Use a Scouting Tool?

Yes. You absolutely need some kind of scouting tool or you will make a lot of inventory mistakes. The reason I am able to make good money on Amazon in such a limited time is that I have the best data possible on my phone screen.

I quickly learned that I have no idea of what people will buy. If I relied on my personal taste and instincts, I would miss out on a ton of good inventory.

You don't need to have a Bluetooth scanner but it really helps. I can zip through a lot more inventory in a shorter time with the Bluetooth scanner. If you don't have the money now, I suggest you save up and buy one when your profits allow. It really makes a difference.

TAKE ACTION!

1. Set up your Amazon Pro Seller and ScanPower accounts.
2. Print off all your contracts and read them. Amazon expects you to know this information and not knowing it can get you into trouble.
3. Set up your ScanPower Mobile account on your smartphone.
4. Connect your Scanfob (if you have one) to your smartphone.
5. Get your books and supplies together in readiness for the next step – your first shipment to Amazon.

11

GO! YOUR FIRST BOX TO AMAZON

Are your accounts set up on Amazon and ScanPower (or whatever listing program you choose)? Then it is time to start listing and pricing your inventory! For simplicity's sake, start with a box of the same type of items (books or CDs or DVDs or video games, for example) so that everything will most likely be going to the same warehouse.

Your box cannot weigh more than 50 pounds when it is shipped, so figure on between 35 and 50 books per box depending on size of box. I'm assuming your first box will be books simply because many people have books around the house they would be willing to sell. These instructions work no matter what kind of inventory you are sending in.

Here's what you will accomplish in this chapter:

1. Set up your USB scanner.
2. Set up your label printer if you have one.
3. Adjust your settings in ScanPower.
4. Set up a naming and numbering system for your inventory.
5. List a box of inventory.

6. Pack and ship your box to Amazon.

SET UP YOUR USB SCANNER

Most USB scanners are "plug and play" which means you only need to plug them in and they work. Plug your handheld scanner into one of the USB ports on your computer.

Most scanners come with a page of different bar codes and numbers. These are test pages and many of the weird-looking ones are for highly specialized applications that you will never use, so ignore them. What you want to do is test your scanner on an ISBN # or UPC code.

1. Open up a word processing file (in MS Word or whatever program you use) and place your cursor at the top of the page.
2. Place the test paper that came with the scanner on your desk and scan from your test sheet. Or grab a book or some other item with a UPC code and scan the barcode.
3. You should hear a beep and a string of numbers will appear at the top of your screen.
4. That's it!

With handheld scanners, you generally have to get pretty close to the item being scanned. With the Bluetooth scanner that you'll use for scouting, you can be far away from the barcode.

Once you are comfortable that your USB scanner is working, move on to the label printer.

SET UP THE LABEL PRINTER

If you don't have a label printer yet, skip to the next section. Amazon will let you print off your labels as part of its Shipping Queue process on sheets of labels – 30 to a page. It is not as efficient as having a Dymo printer, but it works and if you are on a tight budget, that's the way to start.

I'm going to cover the highlights here, but the ScanPower site is quite comprehensive: http://www.scanpower.com/support/printer-setup/. There is a video at http://www.youtube.com/watch?v=1up1DkAZThY that covers setting up your printer as well. You may want to watch it first.

1. The Dymo comes with directions that may be more current than this so look at those first.
2. Plug your label printer into the electrical outlet, but not into the USB port on your computer yet.
3. Load a roll of labels into the printer. The waxy side of the label should be up and the label should be facing down as you feed it through the slot.
4. Use the DVD that came with it to get the Dymo properly installed on your computer.
5. After the software is installed, plug in the Dymo to a USB port on your computer.
6. Once your label printer is working, you will need to tell it two things and then print a test label:
   i. The orientation of the label (landscape)
   ii. The number of the label you will be using.

7. Make sure you are using Firefox as your browser. It is a free download if you don't already have it [www.firefox.com].

8. Go to http://www.youtube.com/watch?v=1up1DkAZThY (or http://www.youtube.com/watch?v=eXdd2s3sv3I if you are a Mac user).

9. ScanPower also has all the instructions and screen shots at http://www.scanpower.com/support/printer-setup/. Don't be confused by the name "FBA Power" that you might see on the screenshots. That was ScanPower's name originally.

10. Follow the directions to adjust your printer settings and print a test label.

11. If the label looks good and only prints on one label, you are done. If the print is too big or too small for the label, you will need to go back to the Formats and Options screen and adjust your settings until the label prints correctly. See the picture below.

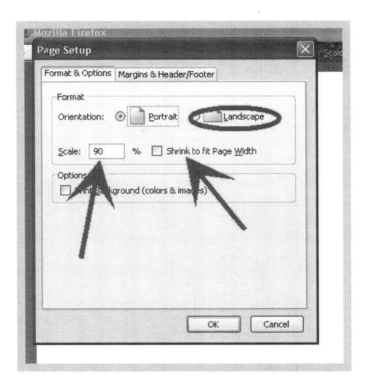

12. You want to make sure the entire text of the label prints on one label, not just the barcode. The two settings in the picture above are the ones that will make the difference.

13. Leave the Firefox tab with the test strip open and click on a new tab to open a new screen.

14. Login to your ScanPower account at http://unity.scanpower.com/.

You may find yourself having to adjust your printer settings from time to time in the future for no particular reason that I can figure out. As long as you know that, you won't panic. Most of the time, all that's needed is to re-select the correct label number you are using and fix the orientation to landscape. Sometimes you have to go through the whole process and adjust the margins and header/footer as well.

ADJUST YOUR SCANPOWER LIST SETTINGS

Now you are almost ready to start using ScanPower to list your inventory and ship it to Amazon's warehouse(s).

I created a seven-page FBA Step-by-Step™with screenshots that walks you through ScanPower's settings for its List program. You can download it/read it here: http://bit.ly/ScanPowerList.

CREATE YOUR INVENTORY NUMBERING AND NAMING SYSTEM

Amazon requires that you have a unique identifier for all merchandise you send to them so that they will always know what inventory at the warehouse is yours. This unique identifier is part of the barcode that is printed on your label printer. Before you process your inventory, you need to create an MSKU.

MSKU (usually pronounced "skew" or "em-skew") stands for "merchant stock keeping unit." It is the numbering system you use for your items. It ties a product and condition together (like a New toy or a Used-Good book) for as long as you choose to send in that item.

In your ScanPower List settings, you have the option of creating a customized MSKU. ScanPower automatically creates a default MSKU for your items that includes the date, the item's ASIN number (Amazon's unique catalog number) and a sequential number (001, 002, 003, etc.).

You can do much, much more and I suggest you do. I use my MSKUs to tell me what I bought (Toys, Books, etc.), where I bought it from (Target, BigLots etc.) and the expiration date (for food items). When I go to reprice my inventory weeks or months later, I can look at the MSKU and quickly know what it is and how long it has been up at the warehouse.

Having the date and location in my MSKU makes it easy for me to hunt down a receipt later if I need to return it or prove to the IRS what I actually paid for it.

In my simple system, I use the date for every item. Not only does this help create a unique identifier for Amazon, but it also allows me to track how long it takes an item to sell and when I first sold a particular item. For example, I have toys that I first shipped in December 2010 and still sell. Every time I scan the toy, the original MSKU comes up and I send in the toy under that MSKU. If you have several copies of the same book, like a Harry Potter, but with different conditions, you will have a unique MSKU for each condition – New, Used-Like New, Used-Very Good, and so on.

Regardless of the name you choose to use for your MSKU, it must end with "_001" or whatever number you want to start with. ScanPower will automatically advance the number with each item you list. Each item MUST have a unique number.

One of the nice features of ScanPower is that not only can you set up your MSKU in settings, but you can customize it on the fly as well. I do that with food items. Because each item of food has a different expiration date, I type that into the MSKU when I am listing the product. I might add "BB 01-24-14" to my MSKU: Oct 5 2013-

GROCERY- BB 01-24-14_001." Later I'll know I bought this food item on October 5th and that it expires January 24, 2014. "BB" stands for "Best By."

LIST YOUR FIRST ITEMS!

Finally! After all the prep and set up, you are ready to list your first items and prepare your first box for Amazon.com!

ScanPower has a brief walk-through of how to use its program here with pictures that you may want to look at in addition to my directions below: http://www.scanpower.com/u2-list-instructions/

1. Grab your first item and your USB scanner.
2. Place your cursor in the screen box on ScanPower that says "UPC, ISBN."
3. Find the barcode and scan your item with your USB handheld scanner.
4. The number should appear in the box that says "UPC, ISBN."
5. A listing will appear on the page for that item.
6. On the pop-up screen, choose your condition (New, Used-Like New, etc.), your quantity and make any changes to your MSKU.
7. You will be taken to another pop-up screen where you can review the data on the product, choose a price and type in what you paid out-of-pocket for that item.

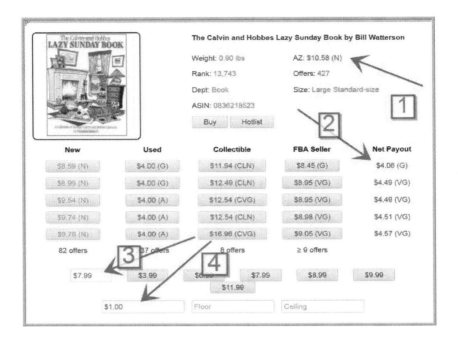

8. You can see that ScanPower gives me a lot of information to make a good decision. At a glance I can see how much Amazon is selling the book for (1) and the net amount of money I would make if I priced my book at $8.45 (2). Since my book is in Used-Acceptable condition, I've priced it a little lower at $7.99 (3). I can keep track of what I paid for the book originally as well (4).

9. If you look at the rank for the book, you will see it is low which means it is selling rapidly. I'll go into pricing and data interpretation in more detail later. For now, I want to focus on creating a listing.

10. Once you have priced your item, the program takes you to the main page.

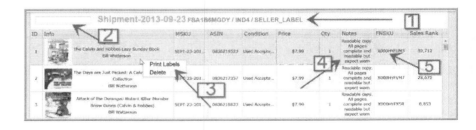

11. Here's what your screen will probably look like. Be aware that software companies are constantly updating and modifying their products. At the top (1) is Amazon's name for your shipment (FBA1B6MGDY), and the warehouse where it is going (IND4=Indiana 4). The empty box is where you need to put your cursor before scanning an item (2). I highlighted the first entry which is why it is darker (3) and also why I can "right-click" my mouse and choose to print or delete this item. All my customized notes are under (4) and the FNSKU is the unique number that Amazon gives me (5) that incorporates my MSKU, condition, pricing – everything.

12. Continue adding items and printing labels. The labels must cover any and all barcodes on the item so that your barcode is the only one that can be read. Sometimes books will have ISBN # and a UPC code. In that case I'll cover one with my label and I'll cover the other with a plain label.

13. If you have notes for some of your items, double-click on the Notes box (number 4 up above) and

choose your pre-written notes or type in unique notes.

14. Be aware that Amazon chooses your warehouse. If you have multiples of an item or items of different sizes, you may find some of your items going to different warehouses.

15. When you have a box ready to go to Amazon, click Complete Shipment at the bottom of the screen.

PACK AND SHIP YOUR BOX TO AMAZON

Now you have at least one box ready to go to Amazon, right? The next step is to pack it up according to Amazon's requirements. If you've read your contract, you already know that you cannot use foam peanuts in your shipment. To fill in gaps in your box and to secure your items, you may use bubble wrap and air pillows as well as clean white paper or clean newsprint (i.e. no ink on it – you can buy it in big rolls). The better and tighter you pack, the less filler you will need.

Leave the box flaps open for now. Weigh your box and write the weight on the flap near the warehouse information – IND4 – 48 lbs. Remember that your box cannot weigh more than 50 pounds. In addition, you need to round up. So if your box is 48 pounds and 8 ounces, for example, round up to 49 pounds.

Back at your ScanPower screen, click on the **Complete Shipment** button. Now you can go to Amazon's Seller Central (http://sellercentral.amazon.com), login and click on Inventory.

Once you are in the inventory screen, you will see in the middle near the top of the page the phrase "Shipping Queue." Click over to the Shipping Queue.

I created a 12-page FBA Step-by-Step with large screenshots for Amazon's Shipping Queue at this link: http://bit.ly/ShippingQueue. It is also in my member site with the updates.

After you are done packing and labeling your boxes, take them to a UPS drop-off location or arrange for UPS to pick up from your location and you are done! Pat yourself on the back!

Your first box will definitely take the longest as you are learning, but you'll be amazed at how fast processing your inventory goes once you are set up. I generally process around 50 unique items an hour (even more if they are multiples). Very soon, you'll be able to fill and ship a box an hour on average.

TAKE ACTION!

1. Set up your USB scanner.
2. Set up your label printer (if you have one).
3. Make sure your settings in ScanPower read the way you want.
4. Determine your own SKU naming system.
5. List, label and ship your first box(es) to Amazon.

6. Note how long it takes them to get to the warehouse(s).
7. Record the first item you sell for posterity!

12

YOUR FIRST SHOPPING TRIP!

Are you ready to go a little nuts? Shopping is the best part of the business. There's nothing quite like finding a super bargain. I've been known to squeal, gasp and jump up and down, depending on who is around me. Some deals are so good, I have to scan them several times to convince myself that they are real. This is the fun part of the business!

My friend Lesley found a super thrift store and we go together when we can for the sheer joy of it. Sometimes it is hard not to run laps around the store when we find a book or DVD for 10 cents and it registers as $30 or $40 on Amazon.

My dad found a discontinued item at Toys "R" Us for $3 that he sold like crazy on Amazon for $65. Yep $65. Stores across the country were sold out and he had the only ones.

At a book sale recently, I was buying cookbooks for $1 in Used-Like New condition which I sold for $9 to $30. Rumplestiltskin has nothing on an FBA seller when it comes to turning straw into gold!

In this chapter, I'll show you how to use ScanPower Mobile while scouting. Most importantly, I'll talk about how to interpret the data so you can make smart buying decisions.

SET UP YOUR SMARTPHONE

As I mentioned in Chapter 10, it is not required to have a Scanfob 2005 to make ScanPower Mobile work. You can enter ISBN#'s manually, use the phone's built-in camera to take a picture of the ISBN# or use the voice-activated function on your phone (most Androids have this as well as the most recent versions of the iPhone).

A free application called Zebra Xing can be accessed from ScanPower Mobile and reads barcodes with the phone's camera. Regardless of whether you have a wireless scanner, you'll occasionally need to enter numbers manually or by voice simply because some items don't have barcodes.

I love having the Scanfob because it makes shopping fast and I have limited time, but it was my biggest hardware expense. If you go to the Frequently Asked Questions on my blog and scroll down, you can get a discount on the Scanfob.

You need a smartphone in order to use the ScanPower Mobile application. This can be an iPhone, an iPad, an iPod touch or a phone with the Android operating system. The phone must have at least 3G, preferably 4G. If you have an unlimited data plan, that's good — just make sure you have a reasonable data plan. AT&T allows 2MG per month, which was more than enough for me until my teenage son joined my plan.

Since I covered how to connect Scanfob to your ScanPower Mobile app in detail in Chapter 10, I won't repeat it here.

INTERPRETING THE DATA

Now that your equipment is working, you are ready to shop. When you arrive at the store, turn on your Scanfob and phone. If you are interested in a slick one-handed scanning assembly, look at Chris Green's Borg-like solution [http://www.screencast.com/t/5cOELqAiP]. Please note that "FBA Scout" was the previous name for ScanPower Mobile. He looks like a Borg, but he can move really fast. You will be assimilated! (Non-trekkers roll your eyes here.)

ScanPower Mobile gives you strategic information:

- Weight and size (makes a difference for textbooks and really heavy items as well as oversize items)
- Rank
- Amazon's price (if Amazon is selling the item)
- Department (Books, Toys, Electronics, etc.)
- New offers from Merchant sellers
- Used offers from Merchant sellers
- Collectible offers
- FBA Sellers
- How many of the item each FBA seller has in stock
- Your net price as an FBA seller

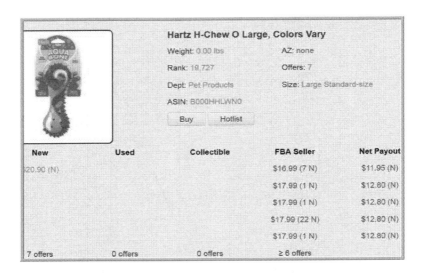

New	Used	Collectible	FBA Seller	Net Payout
$20.90 (N)			$16.99 (7 N)	$11.95 (N)
			$17.99 (1 N)	$12.80 (N)
			$17.99 (1 N)	$12.80 (N)
			$17.99 (22 N)	$12.80 (N)
			$17.99 (1 N)	$12.80 (N)
7 offers	0 offers	0 offers	≥ 6 offers	

I love these dog toys. I bought them for $1.99 and I'm selling several a day for $16.99. Next to each seller's offering price, you see a number in parentheses. That number is how many of the item that seller has for sale. To the right of each FBA seller's offering price, you see another dollar figure. That number represents the seller's net. The net is calculated for you by ScanPower Mobile. It represents what Amazon will send you after commissions and fees are subtracted. You can then subtract your acquisition cost from that number to get a close idea of how much you'll actually make from this item. This number does NOT include your shipping costs to Amazon. If there is no FBA seller, the net calculation will be from a new merchant offer. You can tell the difference because Merchant offers are blue and the net will be blue. Used are red and the net will be red.

In this category you cannot sell used. You can see the blue merchant offer on the left for $20.90. That number actually represents his price *plus* the shipping added in. In other words, his price on Amazon is less than

$20.90, but when you add the shipping, it will cost the customer $20.90 to get it.

Do you begin to see how an FBA seller can make more money than a merchant seller? We can charge more for the same item and get it. In this case, I charged less but that's because there were other sellers to compete against. If it was just me and him, I would have started at $20.99.

This is a tremendous tool for you as a seller. For example, what if the $16.99 seller had 200 units? Would that affect my decision to buy and the price I might sell it at? You bet it would! Now I can see that I would have to price my items lower than the other guy – and to keep lowering it if he keeps lowering it. Because I already know that I sell about three units a day of this product when I am the only seller, a person with 200 units would have at least a six-month supply. I wouldn't want to have to wait until she/he sold out and I wouldn't want to get into a pricing war – so would I still buy it?

In this case, yes. The margin is really good and if I price my items at the _same price_ as the other guy, then I won't trigger a race to the bottom price-wise. In addition, we will rotate through Amazon's Buy Box. I will get my chance in the box and I'll still be able to sell my goods. It won't be as fast as if I was the only one with the $16.99 price, but it will sell.

The Joslin Diabetes Gourmet Cookbook: Heart-Healthy Everyday Recipes For Family And Friends by Polin, Bonnie Sanders

Weight: 2.45 lbs   AZ: none

Rank: 797,379   Offers: 94

Dept: Book   Size: Large Standard-size

ASIN: 0553087606

Buy   Hotlist

New	Used	Collectible	FBA Seller	Net Payout
$28.75 (N)	$4.00 (G)		$14.71 (VG)	$8.95 (VG)
$32.65 (N)	$4.00 (G)		$14.88 (VG)	$9.10 (VG)
$32.65 (N)	$4.00 (G)		$14.97 (VG)	$9.17 (VG)
$32.95 (N)	$4.00 (A)		$17.49 (VG)	$11.32 (VG)
$43.98 (N)	$4.00 (G)		$19.95 (VG)	$13.41 (VG)
15 offers	78 offers	1 offer	≥ 9 offers	

Of course, "Books" is the department in which most people sell. There are over 10.5 million ranked books in Amazon's catalog and the number grows daily at a rate of over 200,000 per year. There are 33.6 million books listed on Amazon, which means that 23.1 million books have not sold a single unit and have no rank. I bought this cookbook for $1. Because it is signed by the author, I'm selling it as Collectible-Like New for $25. I am approved to sell Collectible books. In the beginning I would have sold this as a Used-Like New book.

I see the rank is 797,379 which tells me Amazon hasn't sold this book for a week or two, but it is still in my personal rank criteria.

Now that we've had some fun shopping, let's look at some of the other features of ScanPower Mobile that make my life easier. First, the Buy button. If you decide to buy an item while scouting, click on Buy. When you get back home in front of your computer you can pull up everything you bought this way instantly in ScanPower List. It saves a step. Then you can go back to scanning.

A few other features of ScanPower Mobile:

- The ISBN# screen is where your scanner will put the number. However, if you tap here, you can enter a number manually. This is very helpful for books without a barcode (generally books published before 1980).

- Another way to enter a number is by voice command. Click on the microphone to speak the number into ScanPower Mobile. You need to say the numbers smoothly with no significant pauses. If you do pause, there will be a space in your number that you will have to delete before it will pull up the data properly.
- If you click on the barcode symbol at the top, your phone's camera will activate. Hold your phone over the barcode and let the auto-focus feature of your phone zoom in on the barcode. Once it reads the barcode, the number will appear in the ISBN# screen, as will the data pulled from Amazon. This is a very handy feature if you happen to be out and don't have your scanner with you. You wouldn't want to attend a book sale and scan this way, but it is great for a few items.

By the way, this screenshot is from an older version of ScanPower (originally called FBA Scout) but the latest version has the same features.

To pull it all together, when I go shopping, I scan items in the categories for which I am approved to sell. That means books, DVDs, CDs, video games, collectible games and toys, new toys and games, baby items, sports, kitchen, housewares, electronics, pets, grocery and more.

In the beginning I would scan everything because I had no idea which items would have the right margins coupled with a decent rank. For example, I scanned some kids' Dora the Explorer bike helmets one day which were $8 at BigLots. I was shocked to see that I could sell them for $45 or more on Amazon...and I did! I would not have guessed that. The reason I scanned them was I told myself I would scan like crazy until I got a feel for things.

Today, I have a much better understanding and intuition for brands that are likely to be popular. Because I've scanned so many toys, etc., over the years I can skip some today that I know won't have the margin. Today I scan bike helmets with popular kids' characters on them if they are $10 or less. Today my hit rate is much quicker than when I was first starting. It will be the same for you. There is no substitute for experience.

That being said, I found plenty of things to sell right from the beginning. My first shopping trip was with Chris Green, and I learned from him to shop the whole store. I was stunned to see him put cases of baby wipes into his cart. I would have never thought of scanning butt wipes.

He told me "Moms are particular. If they like a particular brand and it gets discontinued or hard to find, they'll pay a premium to get it."

And he was right! He bought butt wipes for $1.50 a package that he was selling for $25 on line. Nope. That's not a typo. I sold some too!

I bought toys and electronics that first trip. Since then I've bought in nearly every department of BigLots from appliances to beauty to pets to toys to household goods.

BigLots

The first retail store I ever scouted was BigLots. I had never even been inside one before, and I couldn't believe all the brand-name merchandise that was for sale. Grasping my new scanner and smartphone, I waded in.

BigLots mostly sells closeouts in big lots from major manufacturers. That means that when something is gone, it is gone. Only a few items in the store show up month after month. Because the merchandise turns fast, there is good opportunity to find new things. Rarely will you be able to find a large quantity at any given store. If I find something really good, I'll hit all the other stores in my area. Here are the categories where I spend my time:

Toys

There are many brand name toys at BigLots. I've had success with Barbie, Disney-branded items (like "Cars" cars and racetracks or Disney Princess accessories), Dora, SpongeBob, Sesame Street, Matchbox, action figures and *some* Fisher-Price (a lot of FP is the same price on Amazon). Sometimes you have to wait for a sale to make it worthwhile. Many FBA sellers shop at BigLots, so sometimes they'll push down the prices, which is annoying and unnecessary. I keep that in mind when I buy – I may have to wait if people jump in later. I won't buy if there are already several FBA folks selling it.

One holiday season I bought about 20 of the new ethnic Barbies (they were all wearing black) for $8 each on sale and sold them for $24-$27 each. I am usually able to find items where I can price at least 3X higher than my cost.

During the off-season, toys can be dismal since the dogs from the holidays are still on the shelves. The managers don't put out very much new stuff when the shelves are still full, nor do they take in new toys from HQ until they are out of what is on their shelves. Some stores will reduce the number of shelves devoted to toys after the holidays as well. This is one of the few exceptions to my statement above about fast turnover. It can slow down a lot in toys unless you are in a store that has many families with young kids.

Pets

I've sold everything I ever bought in the pet category and quickly. I've had success with everything from poop bags to toys to training tools to leashes to food.

Baby

I love the baby category. BigLots has been my source for a lot of spoons, bowls, diaper bags, nipples, butt wipes, booster chairs and pacifiers. The tricky thing with pacifiers is to make sure you are looking at the right ones on Amazon – many of them share the same UPC code.

One booster chair cost $19 (I often bought them with 25% discounts) and sold for around $50. When I had them in stock, I sold at least one a day, usually two or three. I was the only seller for a very long time. I miss those chairs. I drove all over the Metroplex to get them.

Home Goods

I've had success with bedding and some branded decorative items as well as organizational tools. Again, think about brand name recognition when scanning in this category. I've sold high-ranking items lickety-split when there were no other FBA sellers, so I can't really tell you what a good rank is in this category. I look for brand and cuteness factor or usefulness.

I went all over the Metroplex picking up Harley Davidson comforter sets that I was buying for $25 and selling for $124-$140. They sold out within days of every order I sent in.

Appliances

My Dad turned me on to this category at BigLots. The trick in appliances is to find that high-end luxury brand.

A year or so ago, a huge shipment of refurbished Cuisinart appliances hit the stores nationwide and several of them were tremendous sellers. Very few FBA sellers scanned this category or perhaps they were put off by the somewhat high purchase price, I don't know, but appliances were one of my best sellers overall. The Cuisinarts were mostly coffee makers. I found a particular pressure cooker for about $39 (depending on discount/sale or coupon that I had) that sold for $135 as quick as I could ship them to Amazon. A particular style of slow cooker was selling for $24 at BigLots and on Amazon for $75-$79. I did not care that they were big!

Grocery

I've recently gotten into this category in a big way thanks to Jessica Larrew's *Liquidation Gold* book (see resources in the back of the book or on my website at:

http://www.sellstepbystep.com for more details). I've found some items worth selling at BigLots. Again, you are looking for a well-known brand. Be aware that Amazon will pull items that are 60 days from expiration. Give yourself plenty of time to sell before it is pulled.

DVDs/CDs

There are sometimes great sellers at BigLots for only $3, $5, $7 or $10 (depending on if they are sets or not). The big problem is the!#$%! stickers. You have to peel away the white stickers they use to cover the barcode, which can be very tedious. What I look for are brand-new sets like Season 1 of... or collections of movies Best Horror...etc. They tend to be the ones I can sell for $27-$35.

One day I happened to be in the section when an employee opened a brand-new box of DVDs. It was a collection of five movies about lawyers (go figure). I took the entire box for $7 each and sold each of them for around $45. I can't tell you how many seasons of 7th Heaven I sold where I bought them for $3 or $5 (depending on the store) and sold them for $27.

I was burned on Twin Peaks, though. I bought too many and may never sell them for a reasonable price.

I also look for old movies that might be hard to find. Don't bother with the blockbusters like Spiderman or anything with an action star in it.

Skip all the kiddy movies and Nickelodeon cartoons. They're oversaturated and not even worth $3 on Amazon. I found success with the original Airbender and a couple of other anime series (not to be confused with cartoons).

Beware! BigLots has started selling used sets from Blockbusters and other video stores now and they are wrapped up like new. Take a close look and make sure you are buying new or that the margin is still good enough if it is used.

Seasonal

I've had luck with tool-type items and gardening, but not holiday stuff. I'll still wander over and scan from time to time, but there generally aren't brand items in this category that sell.

Electronics

It took me a while to ease into this category, largely because Amazon doesn't monitor rank on all of its electronics. I'd look at my phone and wonder if the rank was blank because it had never sold a unit or because it was in electronics. I finally waded in with some brand name electronics and designer stuff. I sold many Monster High headsets, DSi cover sets, etc. I've sold everything I've ever bought pretty quickly. I've had Amazon undercut me on a number of hot games and Wii accessories, though, so I've learned to send in no more than 4-5 at a time. If the item is ranked and it is less than 1000, you can bet Amazon will sell it for less than you will in the future.

Sometimes I bought stuff where it said Amazon was not selling it. I realized later that Amazon *was* selling it but they happened to be out when I was looking at my scanner. That happens on really hot toys and electronics more often than I would like.

Rewards Program

BigLots has a decent rewards program. Signup at: www.biglots.com or at the store. If you sign up online, they'll have your card waiting for you at the store. You'll want to sign up in advance if you can. The checkers at BigLots are SLOW with keying in stuff.

If you have 10 different shopping trips with each trip spending more than $20, they'll give you 20% off a shopping trip of your choosing. Needless to say, I buy BIG when I have the discount. In addition, they offer that 20% off as a coupon to their Rewards members about four-five times a year even if you've not yet earned it. You get weekly sales notices from them by email so you can do some scouting before going to the store.

The one bummer about their program is that you can't always use your sales tax certificate with it. It seems to vary from store to store whether or not they will let you. So, if I choose to buy tax-free, I sometimes have to come back home, login to the rewards program and then register my sale manually. It is a hassle. If I have 20% off, I don't also get the sales tax off in some stores. I think this is a mistake on their part since sales tax is no skin off their nose, but no one asked me.

Also, if you register in a store for no sales tax it is 1) a HUGE hassle and 2) only good in that store. You can't just show your certificate; you have to register at every store. If you are like me and shop 4-5 BigLots regularly, it is enough to make you want to kill yourself. For that reason, I rarely use my sales tax certificate at a BigLots. If you only have one or two in your town, then go for it. Wait until there is no one in line. It will take 15-20 minutes at least because they'll have to find a manager, and it will have to be re-entered a couple of times. I swear I'm not exaggerating.

Goodwill

Thrift stores are a great source of inventory for FBA sellers and it is an adventure every time in more ways than one. Goodwill is a slightly different beast than the typical neighborhood thrift store. For one thing, Goodwill is a huge organization with locations all over North America including Canada and Mexico. What does this mean to you? It means they tend to be really well organized with warehouses and the ability to distribute huge lots of goods across a large region.

If this sounds a bit like BigLots, it should. Goodwill gets new and slightly damaged merchandise in large lots from businesses and manufacturers of all kinds. The organization balances out where the goods go so no one store is overwhelmed by a particular item. It may even spread a large lot across multiple regions which means that other Goodwill shoppers across the country might have the same item, not just local stores.

If you find a good seller in one Goodwill near you, it is likely that you can pick up more at another Goodwill. These are brand new items although sometimes the boxes are beat up and not good for selling. Often Amazon is no longer (or never did) selling these items because they are discontinued, which is also nice for us. A preponderance of new Goodwill items sell between $2 and $6.

Of course, the majority of inventory at Goodwill is used, donated items from individuals and small groups. These items are collected either at individual stores or collection sites throughout the city. They are sorted (lots of stuff is trashed on the spot – you'd be amazed at the garbage some people donate) and often taken to a central warehouse where the goods are balanced out. My local Goodwills, for example, are full of used textbooks right now – most of them only $2 – and I'm seeing some repeats from store to store. I've bought entire shopping carts full of textbooks with under 1 million rankings and I'm thrilled. I can only speculate where they got them because normally you'd only see a few textbooks at a Goodwill and yet the past couple of weeks have been staggering.

By the way, the reason you only see a few textbooks at many Goodwills is because many of them are now selling their more valuable books on Amazon! Because each region is under different management, you see a lot of Goodwills selling online. Their competency in selling is highly variable and they don't have the manpower to plow through all the books they get, but textbooks usually get some scrutiny. They are easy to pick out of a pile for one thing.

Which brings me to the question, what can you buy at a Goodwill to sell on FBA? Unlike eBay, there are many categories on Amazon where you can ONLY sell new items like Baby and Toys, so be sure you know what can be sold used, what can be sold collectible and what can be sold Open Box. If you aren't sure, look it up in the Help section of Seller Central. Amazon is very clear.

One thing you can't really anticipate is the "who is forbidding us to sell now?" question. Some manufacturers have clout with Amazon and restrict third-party sellers of their goods. I bought some new party plates at Target with Cars 2 on them. I found out after a couple of weeks of selling them that I could no longer sell them. Ironically, the matching napkins were no problem and I sold all of those. The plates came back to me, and I'm selling them through another channel. Amazon doesn't publish a list or anything you can check, so this is how most people find out that they can't sell something that looked so great on the scanner. You can call Amazon before listing a product if you are concerned – this was the solution they offered me when I asked what we sellers could do.

If you see an item with no FBA sellers, which is clearly branded, be aware that it might end up being something you have to merchant-fulfill or sell in another category. I just bought a brand-new Disney iPhone case for $2 at Goodwill. There are merchant but no FBA sellers. I suspect it might end up going the eBay route or merchant-fulfilled, but I couldn't resist the deal. They sell new from Disney for around $30.

So here's how I work a Goodwill:

- **Stuff up front in bins or on display shelves** – This is often the new merchandise they are trying to move. I bought new sports goods and toys recently from bins up front.
- **Books** – I'm looking for non-fiction for the most part.
- **Collectible Games** – the exception to the rule that all toys must be new is if it is a collectible, meaning it is discontinued, old, rare, hard-to-find. Another clue is that Amazon is not selling it either. If they are selling it, it is definitely not collectible. Bring a small knife to open any tape and make sure all the pieces are there before you leave or that they are easy and cheap to replace like timers, clay, dice, etc. You have to sell complete games. At some Goodwills they will let you bring incomplete games back, but _most of them don't_ so be sure to check for pieces.
- **New merchandise hidden in the kitchen/appliance area** – air filters, designer napkins, vacuum cleaner bags...who knew?

- **Allowable used appliances**. In one of his eBooks, Jordan Malik (see "resources" later in the book) turned me on to Sharper Image air purifiers and how people will buy them used and in a box of my own making (they are oddly shaped). With the exception of large items like this, I personally only buy products that are in their original packaging even if they clearly used. It saves me creating a box and is more appealing to potential customers to buy an "open box" item. Be sure to plug in any appliances before you leave the store and check that they are working.

- **VHS tapes** – new, sealed in plastic, only. Don't bother with used from a Goodwill, most are in terrible shape and will only bring you negative feedback. Also, make sure there is really good margin on the tape. VHS sell slowly and you want to make sure your margin can afford a year or so worth of storage fees if it comes to that. You want tapes that aren't available on DVD and are rare and hard to find.

- **Computer software and games** – used is fine. Make sure the discs look very clean. If you're doubtful, don't buy it. If you are looking at a jewel case and there is no barcode on it, the software/video game originally came in a box, probably with other stuff like a booklet. You cannot sell it without the box and original stuff.

- **DVDs** – you probably won't find much of value in this section since people tend to donate their unwanted DVDs (translate=blockbusters that everyone has) so it is usually last on my list EXCEPT if it is brand new, sealed in package. Then I'll check it out. With Roku and iTunes, fewer and fewer people are buying DVDs so keep the rank low (I suggest under 10,000 but this is not a hard and fast rule and other sellers may disagree with me).

- **Stuffed animals** – usually stuffed animals are piled up on top of clothing racks. I've occasionally found brand new toys with their original tags that show no wear whatsoever. I found two Harley Davidson branded toys this way. I suspect they were protected rather than played with which was great for me. Some toys will have matted fur or worn tags. These are not new and you can't sell them. If they smell like cigarettes or cats, don't sell them. In Amazon's world, "New is New" and not "nearly" or "mostly" new. You can sell collectible toys so if the stuffed animal is in excellent shape without a smell; it may be worth looking up to see if it is a discontinued toy. I found several discontinued Eeyore's in Collectible-Like New condition at thrift stores recently that are selling for $30-$40 online (I paid $2 or less).

- **Baby items** – must be new. Boxes must look great. Don't pick up a slightly dinged or scratched box. Moms are very picky. It is not worth the grief. Be aware of items that are not sellable like crib bumpers and check all butt wipes and diapers to see what size package they are sold in. Most times what I find at Goodwill is not enough to sell on Amazon (like there are 12 packages in a case kind of thing). Don't sell formula or food unless the expiration is more than 6 months out.

- **High-dollar items** – usually there is a locked case somewhere with higher priced items in excellent condition. These might be collectibles, new items or even auction items (i.e. you have to bid to win them). They'll let you scan while they watch. You can find some very nice things in the case like expensive digital cameras, collectible comic books and more.

Things to know:

1. Sale items and books are not returnable in most Goodwills and thrift stores. They get so many books – they do NOT want them back.
2. Books and other departments will go on sale fairly regularly.
3. Some Goodwills are so organized they have "clubs" with membership cards, discounts, special sales...just like any typical retailer. Sign up, they're worth it. I'm a member of the Goodwill group that covers West Chicago up to Central Wisconsin. Why? Because my friend Lynn lives there, and we go shopping together when I visit.
4. You will need to sign up with each Goodwill separately with your sales tax certificate *unless* it is one of those highly organized and technologically interconnected groups (like the Chicago area). In most cases, they three-hole punch your form and put it in a notebook to check against next time. I'm not kidding. In North Texas, we're lucky the cash registers don't use pop-up numbers. It is ironic since we're in the Telecom Corridor.

As a special caveat, I will warn you that part of Goodwill's mission is to train unskilled and formerly homeless people for jobs. Often the person behind the counter is close to illiterate and finds a cash register intimidating. Things like ringing up your purchase as non-taxable can be a problem. Checking out with multiple shopping carts can be a problem. Finding your sales tax certificate in the 3-ring notebook can be a problem. Be patient and cheerful and remember this is *normal* and part of the mission. Checkout for me can take half an hour sometimes.

This caveat applies to a lot of non-profit thrift stores, not just Goodwill of course. Salvation Army is also an excellent resource. I don't know about the rest of the country, but they are not quite as organized down here as Goodwill. You have to go to the right neighborhood to find the real finds for Salvation Army, whereas I find the Goodwills to be fairly consistent throughout a region. In terms of working the store, I pretty much work them all the same.

Many thrift stores have special sale days each month or special sections of the store on sale (like books). When my Mom is in town, we go shopping together to take advantage of her senior citizen discount. Some move inventory like crazy, some have the same old stuff every time. Your mission is to find the stores with swift turnover and visit regularly. One thrift store I know of discounts books to 10 cents on Saturdays and their turnover is very fast. It is a dirty, crowded hole-in-the-wall but an excellent find for an FBA scout.

If you would like to learn more about thrifting from other FBA sellers, Chris Green has videos that he records live of some of his shopping trips. ScanPower has a YouTube channel with episodes like "Thrifting with the Boys" and "Thrift Store Haul with Chris Green at the Salvation Army." In addition, there is a regular internet radio show (with archives!) called "Thrifting for Profit – The Amazon Way" with Debra Conrad and "Thrifting-with-the-Boys" with Jason Smith that you may find interesting. These folks thrift for both eBay and Amazon so some of the items they find (like designer clothes) may not be appropriate for Amazon FBA sellers. Go to: http://www.makethosandsupdates.com for the latest links.

IKEA

I love IKEA in a weird psycho-fan kind of way. I have been to the opening day of four IKEAs as they expanded into the US. I ran through the gauntlet of screaming Swedes to grab those opening day specials. They have special "beaters" that make it even louder and more exciting when you enter. I've spent days of my life in IKEA wandering the aisles. I gushed over the showrooms. I ate the meatballs (before I went vegetarian). I know all the secret passages and all the sections like I designed them myself. I've shopped IKEA on two continents. IKEA is the number one furniture retailer *in the world* (yep, it came to the US *late* in its world conquest. It is more than 60 years old).

So how come I didn't think about IKEA for FBA until recently? Well, partly because it is a store that exclusively sells its own brand. I know they have an online site and I just assumed that you couldn't buy IKEA on Amazon. I also erroneously thought that no one would want to pay premium prices on something that was so cheap in the store. Boy was I wrong! So keep that in mind when you are scouting. *Everything* is a possibility to sell on Amazon. The second thought was really just dumb because I buy cheap stuff in stores like Target, Wal-Mart and BigLots and sell it for a premium all the time on

Amazon, but IKEA is so well known for its low prices...well, I was just wrong.

Naturally with an excuse to shop at IKEA, I had to go. My friend Denny Gaye and I arrived at 10 and left at 4 tired but triumphant. Here's what I learned in a nutshell:

There are no barcodes – you have to type everything into ScanPower Mobile or whatever you are using to scout. Their barcodes are unique to IKEA so you have to use product names to search. I used the phrase "IKEA + insert weird Swede name" to look it up on Amazon. This slows down the process, obviously and you have to be picky about what you investigate. It went faster with the two of us dividing and conquering.

Make sure to check the size – I fell in love with a particular lamp. The margin was great, I was all over it. When I went to actually pick up the lamp, I realized there were two sizes of pendant lamp (hanging lamps) and two prices, naturally. I had to surf through the Amazon listing to figure out that the price was actually for the bigger, more expensive lamp. Now all of a sudden the margin was lousy. It was depressing, but it made me more cautious for the rest of the trip to make sure I was truly looking at the right listing on Amazon.

Not everything has a rank – I noticed that many of the products didn't have a rank yet. This could be because they were so newly added to the catalog that they've not sold yet. For new sellers, I recommend buying products with rank because you can be sure that they have sold before. However, if you are willing to take the risk, go ahead and list your stuff without it. I saw a LOT of merchant sellers, and I think that was their strategy. If it doesn't sell, it is easy to return since it is in their house instead of at Amazon's warehouse. I have no room in my house, so that strategy doesn't work for me.

Not everything has a seller – This was interesting, too. We saw products without any sellers and I can only conclude that they were out – all products had sold – or the merchant sellers had returned their items. If I saw no rank and no sellers, I usually put it back down. If I saw rank but no sellers, I looked more closely.

Not everything is for sale – There are scads of IKEA products *not* for sale on Amazon. If you think they should be and are willing to add new items to the Amazon catalog, go for it. I didn't do that this time, but I might in the future. It generally takes me about half an hour to 45 minutes to add a new product to Amazon's catalog so I'll only do it if I have a lot to sell. There were several things I thought should be for sale on Amazon and that would be popular.

There are some stupid prices out there – All I can guess is that most of the FBA sellers with IKEA products don't have ScanPower because I saw some of the dumbest prices ever. People were spending $40 to make $10 after Amazon's fees. I could only conclude that these low-ball sellers were not aware of how much Amazon's fees would actually be. While IKEA packs things into nice flat boxes, the fact is some of them are still oversized and the fees can be a lot. I put down some items for that reason. Amazon's fees were so high, it just didn't make sense. I saw a gorgeous $49 lamp I wanted to sell for $200 but everyone else was selling it around $100. It didn't make sense. The oversize fees were nearly $50. Because there were so many lowball sellers, I decided to wait until my next trip to check it out again. I looked at lingonberry jam and other specialty foods and I have no idea why the prices were so low on Amazon. It didn't make sense to spend $4 and clear $1 after expenses. Where the heck does anyone buy lingonberries in the US? I'll check again when I go back to see if the crazy sellers are gone.

Eat lunch – the place is massive. You'll get tired. Have lunch. This place takes stamina. Wear comfortable shoes, too.

Think about the buyer – who buys IKEA on Amazon? My guess is someone who is far away from an IKEA but who is familiar with their merchandise; someone who is super busy and doesn't want to lose a day in IKEA Wonderland; someone who hates to shop but loves Allen wrench projects; a designer or someone else who appreciates modern design in a big way. All of the above. Kind of like Amazon Prime buyers, people who shop at IKEA really love it. It has a cult following. Your buyer is a fan and fans want what they want. Remember that.

What can they only buy from IKEA? – Again, you don't want to sell something simple like a black picture frame that they can get anywhere. You want something that can only be bought at IKEA, and that is cool and desirable. I looked at bedding, pillows, curtains, lamps, rugs, toys, small furniture, shelving and certain chairs. IKEA's wonderful graphics, cool design, kitchen wonders and unique chic are apparent in these items. If you find yourself saying, "that is so cool!" then it is probably a sellable item.

Why would they buy from you? – As I mentioned, IKEA sells online, too. However, their shipping costs are really high and it can take three weeks or more to get your stuff when you buy online from them. Amazon offers Prime buyers free 2-day shipping or overnight for a little bit more. It's no contest. Prime buyers are 1) more affluent and 2) impatient. In addition, IKEAs are not ubiquitous like a Target or Wal-Mart. They very carefully select their sites based on a certain population level. While there are three

IKEAs in the New York tri-state metropolitan area for example, there are only three IKEAs in all of Texas (DFW, Houston & Austin area).

Join the Club – IKEA has a new club called IKEA FAMILY. You'll see low prices throughout the store that are only available to club members. You can join at the kiosk near check-out and use your card immediately. It is worth it. I saved almost $60 right off the bat. Naturally, they will market to you relentlessly for life, but you want to know when their sales are, right? You also get a free coffee or tea in the café every time you visit to take the sting out of it. They send you monthly deals that are exclusive to club members and the discounts can be substantial. They also offer you 90-day price protection if you are member. If your item goes down in price in the next 90 days, you can get the difference.

Shop Ahead of Time – Once you are a member of the club, you can login and shop the monthly deals before you go to the store. Since you have to enter them into ScanPower by name no matter what, might as well do that at home with your high-speed internet and save your feet. You can look at all the IKEA inventory on Amazon simply by keying in "IKEA" in the search bar and then you can sort by category.

Note the tags – if you are not used to shopping at IKEA, you need to understand that you pick up a lot of the items from the top floor in the warehouse section of the bottom floor. If you find a coffee table or something that works out, take a picture of the red tag or write down where to find it in the warehouse downstairs. It will save you time later.

Use ScanPower Mobile's "Buy" Button – In addition, if I find something I want, I push the "Buy" button on ScanPower Mobile. This way I don't have to search for the product again later when I want to list the products and process my inventory. I can simply pull up my buy list into ScanPower's List program all ready for me to add prices and print labels.

Get a flatbed – Again, if you are not familiar with the store, when you get to the warehouse section, they will have flatbed carts for you on your immediate left. Be sure to grab one. It is much easier to put your boxes on a flatbed than to try and cram them into a cart.

No price tags, no extra packaging – Most items are nicely packed in a compact box perfect for sending to Amazon's warehouse. There are no stickers to remove and the boxes are well-packed and durable enough for Amazon's warehouse. You still need to place them inside of a bigger box, of course. Be sure to cover IKEA's barcodes or anything that looks like a barcode.

Discounts for cash, checks or debit – I don't know if this is everywhere like the new Club, but IKEA offers small discounts if you use cash, checks or debit and sometimes they'll also give you a discount on your *next* purchase if you do this. In my case the other day, I used my debit card as credit for the extra buyer's protection it gives me so I didn't get that particular benefit.

Know what sells – If you are a long-time IKEA fan like me, you'll know there are certain chairs, tables, toys, kids accessories, etc. that have been there *forever.* Why is this? Because they are IKEA's best sellers! Poäng chairs will never die! These are items that out-of-towners might well crave. Obviously if you are new, you'll just have to go with your instinct. It would take a year to scan the whole store. Even so, anything that you see year after year in the catalog should make you think. You are getting the catalog aren't you? You will after you sign up for the Club, but you can also get one for free at the customer service section near check-out. Anything that doesn't say "New!" is probably a steady-eddy seller. Anything not in a fad color is probably a steady-eddy.

Get a map – The place is enormous. You can get a map as you come in that will tell you important things like where to find the bathrooms and café, and where to find the secret passages that allow you to cut through sections quickly to get to check-out.

Bring a friend – I was glad I had Denny Gaye with me. Not only was it more fun, we were able to help each other grab boxes, push our three carts, investigate more items together and we had a nice lunch. If I were to describe IKEA in a few words, it would be "furniture amusement park." It is fun, entertaining, and exhausting. There are often long lines at check out. Bring a friend if you can.

Mobile apps – for you techno-weenies (you know who you are) the free IKEA iPhone and Android apps show about 1000 out of the 10,000 products in the IKEA catalog. This is IKEA's way of telling you what its most popular products are.

Shopping list – You can browse online and IKEA will create a printable shopping list for you to bring with you to the store – very nice. A related online service lets you check availability of items before you go. Want more of those great lamps? Make sure they are in stock before you drive a long way for nothing.

No bags – IKEA will happily sell you a shopping bag but they don't offer any at check out. Either bring your own, pay 59 cents for one of theirs (they are very big and blue) or struggle without one for your smaller items.

Babysitting at Småland – They have a special area where you can drop off your kids with professional daycare people. I don't know how much they charge. It may be free. It is very cute. If you are forced to bring your small fry with you, this provides you with some peace while scouting. Leave them at home if you can. IKEA is BIG and super boring for the kids. They put toys and play areas in each section, but still.

Results – It has been a couple of weeks since I got my IKEA order in and so far it has been very interesting and encouraging. Certain items sold very quickly and I'm going back to get more. I bought some $2 kitchen items I'm selling for $12+ and they are flying out of the warehouse. Some of the toys and lamps I bought haven't sold yet, but I'm not worried: I'm waiting for some low-ball sellers to clear the decks. I might even buy their products and resell them. By the way, I did not buy the Poäng chairs this time around. They are big with higher fees and the margin wasn't there with the FBA competition I saw. I'll check again later.

Target

My friend Lynn wrote this post for me about Target. With her help, I've become a much better shopper at Target, and now I take others on Target shopping trips. My comments are italicized:

Today I've asked my friend Lynn Rafter to tell us about scouting at Target. You may have read part of her story in my book. I never thought of Target as a great outlet for inventory until Lynn introduced me to some hot toy deals this past holiday season. Even though the season has passed, she still sells a lot of Target merchandise every week. She uses ScanPower Mobile on her Android phone to help her find the most profitable deals. She sells new items exclusively.

Hi there, I wanted to give you all a few tips and ideas on how to pull profit out of a Target, or any big-box retailer. Even though there may not be tremendous sales going on (just wait until November!) there's always profit to be made shopping at these stores.

Before you go, don't forget your Target credit card, which gives you 5% off all purchases. Bring your sales tax ID #, and coupons, too. Target has coupons on Target.com, and they take manufacturers' coupons.

I buy toys, video games and small housewares. I mostly sell toys because I LOVE TOYS! I can spend hours analyzing the toy section of a store (just ask my family), learning about the merchandise and figuring out what is a hot seller.

One reason I shop Target is because they focus on hot selling items! They have limited shelf space and will quickly dump items that don't sell well. Go ahead and scan almost any item, and you will see that it ranks high on Amazon. Your job is to find the item that will bring you the maximum amount of profit, regardless of whether it is on clearance, discounted or selling for full price.

Electronics

When I shop Target, I start in the electronics section. I hit all of the clearance areas, and each Target usually has an electronics clearance section located one or two aisles away. Scan all the items marked clearance; you will be surprised at what sells at Target for $14.95 may be selling on Amazon for $65.

While I'm in this section, I will scan the merchandise for new items. Many times Target carries items before Amazon, and you can make a nice profit scooping up a few games or electronics for full price that are selling for 3X–4X that on Amazon. Be cautious though.

I usually don't send up more than three of any item if I am unsure of whether it will sell or not.

Toys

Next, I head into Toys. Target usually has multiple clearance toy sections and will have good discounts on toys throughout the department. I have shopped Target so many times I am immediately aware of new merchandise and always scan new items to see what they are retailing for on Amazon. Again, new items at Target may not be available on Amazon, so you could make a nice profit before Amazon gets a chance to sell it at a lower price. Again, don't be put off by the retail price. You never know!

If you find an item at Target that is on clearance and will make a nice profit for you, check out the other Targets in your area, as they usually have the same items on clearance. Be aware though, one Target may list a video game on clearance for $4.95 and another Target will clearance the same game for $14.95. Even though all Targets carry roughly the same items, they set different prices based on the store location.

Double-check all prices before purchasing, and don't feel too bad about returning items that don't fit your margins; Target has a great return policy. You can even return items without a receipt if you have the credit card with which you purchased it.

Target Exclusives

One thing you should look for is the "Only at Target" sticker. Items with this sticker are exclusives and not available to be purchased by Amazon. They are usually only sold by FBA sellers on Amazon for a nice margin. You can do this too!

If you find something that you'd like to sell, please do not get into a race to the bottom price war with other FBA sellers. Know what you need to price your item at to get the return you need. With Target exclusives, there is no reason to go nuts – your units will sell because there are no others. Amazon won't come in and compete with you; you are only cutting your own prices for no reason. This race to the bottom strategy hurts all FBA sellers, and customers come to expect everything to sell cheaply no matter what – it is no way to run a successful business, believe me!

Stick to Brands

Another bit of advice that I follow is to stick to name-brand items. Target and other stores carry items that are private label, meaning that Target has developed this product to be sold only at their stores. Wal-Mart does this a lot, too. Although less expensive than its national brand version, it will have a generic name and label. Think Thomas the Tank Engine, a name-brand item, vs. something like Toot Toot Train, a name that means nothing to most Amazon customers. The generic version is cute in the store, but Amazon customers won't buy it.

Trust Your Instincts

I will spend the rest of my scouting trip looking at baby items and small housewares. I look for anything that has a recognizable face (Elmo, Hello Kitty, Sponge Bob, etc.), is on clearance, or just seems to be wrongly priced. After a while, you will be able to guesstimate in your head what you think an item should be selling for. If you see an electronic baby toy that retails for $7.95 and you think would sell for much higher, go ahead and scan it. Odds are you're right! Target carries many baby must-haves that are luxury items, at a low price.

Amazon customers don't shop at Target as much as I do, and are happy to pay a higher price for the convenience and great service from Amazon.

Hope this helps you navigate around Target more efficiently. Have fun and make money.

Toys "R" Us

This was another guest post from my Dad. My comments are italicized:

I have another great guest blogger for you this week — my Dad. You read some of his story in my book. In this post he goes into more detail about how he makes Toys "R" Us work for him. Dad lives in a small town in North Carolina and yet he has built a successful business for himself by carefully shopping at the few stores he has. He sells a mixture of books and media and new toys and other items. He works his business part-time around a very busy schedule of board meetings and church service and still makes thousands of dollars. My Dad's a planner. See what he did to ensure his success right from the beginning. With no further ado, here's Phil Stine:

Until I became an Amazon FBA seller, I had probably never been in a Toys "R" Us more than three times in my life. But I knew that toys would be a big part of my Christmas profits as well as a steady year-round source of income (kids have birthdays all year long). Last August I went to my local store and asked for the manager. When I eventually found him, I asked him what he thought big sellers would be for Christmas. (I didn't tell him I was going to resell things.) He very kindly spent half an hour showing me what he thought would be big, and where they were on the shelves. Looking back, he was remarkably accurate on what would be popular.

This gave me a good orientation to the layout of the store, and this knowledge was very valuable when I later came in with discount coupons and flyers in hand for some very popular items. All Fisher-Price items are together and arranged by age; all Lego toys are together; remote control items filled up one complete aisle; all X-Box programs were in one area, and so on. I learned very quickly also where the Bratz Dolls were; where the Barbie dolls were; where the Justin Bieber dolls were; where I could find the dollhouses or karaoke machines. When there's a great one-day price on a hot item, you can't afford to waste time trying to find a clerk to point you in the right direction. Some little old grandmother will beat you to the item every time.

While there, I signed up for the Toys "R" Us Rewards card. This gave me advance notice of some sales, but most of all gave me many discount coupons over the months.

Most of the year, there's one flyer a week from Toys "R" Us, giving discounts for that week. Getting into the Christmas season, one feature of these was that they included a coupon with a big discount for a very large number of items from 3:00 pm Friday through 1:00 pm Saturday only. I generally checked these prices and rankings on Amazon before I went to the store and circled the ones that looked like I could sell for three times what I would pay. Then about 2:00 o'clock Friday afternoon, I'd head for those items, scan them to be sure of ranking and price, and fill up my cart ready for checkout at 3:00. Even now, well after Christmas, I do the same with the weekly flyers. I generally go the first day of the flyer, and go first to the items I've circled as being potentially profitable. Having put those in my cart, I then do more of a browse of other items that are discounted or which I know have been pretty popular. There are always some pleasant surprises, but I have to get to the toys in the flyer before other customers.

Occasionally Toys "R" Us will put out discontinued items at large discounts. I found a big stack of discontinued X-Box 360 Guitar Controllers that had originally retailed for $45, and were now marked down to $4.50, except with my discount coupons I got some for $3.75. As I took all the ones they had out, they would bring out a few more the next day, and I'd take those. I eventually bought about 30 of these, none for more than $4.50, and sold them all for $65! **Every single one of them sold—and sold within days of being listed on Amazon**. Here's the lesson: the store wants to bring in the new, but buyers may not care if it's last year's model. You can really profit from that.

Thanksgiving Day, Toys "R" Us opened up at 9:00 p.m. The flyers with special prices for that night were good only until 11:00 am the next day, but they were so good I braved the crowd. The line wrapped around the building by 8:00 that night, but I eventually got in and went directly to my circled items. Some were gone already, but I kept at it until I was ready to check out about 12:30 am. The checkout line snaked through the baby section of the store – I didn't get out until after 3:00 am. However, I had $1500 worth of toys, which I sold for over $4500. I went back the next morning to clean up the less popular items. This year my wife will be with me, so we can fill up three or four carts. I never in my life would have thought that at age 68, I'd be shopping at Toys "R" Us at 3:00 in the morning, but my checks from Amazon.com for

November and December were almost $17,000, so I it was worth it.

I didn't sell everything I bought. In January I was a little discouraged as I still had quite a bit of inventory with Amazon. In the past few weeks, things have begun to pick up, and many of those toys are moving out of the warehouse now. Thank goodness for birthdays. I still make my weekly visit to Toys "R" Us. It's going to be a good year.

Now when Dad goes to Toys "R" Us, the manager and store clerks help him out. They know who he is, and they are happy to bring more units out from the back, watch his carts while he continues to shop and bring out flatbed dollies if he needs them. This comes from building relationships with the store—something I highly recommend. I'm treated like royalty at BigLots and my local Tuesday Morning for the same reason.

Dad has a process and a plan, which makes shopping Toys "R" Us profitable and manageable for him. Consider how you might approach your local stores for maximum efficiency.

Tuesday Morning

One of my favorite stores for scouting for Amazon FBA inventory is Tuesday Morning. Unlike traditional overstock stores, Tuesday Morning focuses on luxury brands. It doesn't sell seconds or imperfect goods, which makes it a great source for scouting. While most items will be last year's models, they are still popular on Amazon. Another feature that makes it a good resource is that each store is different. While some of the merchandise may be the same everywhere, quite often you will find things in one store that don't appear in others nearby. This means there is less likely to be competition from other FBA sellers.

Tuesday Morning is very welcoming for resellers like us. For example, if you find an item you like, you can call in to 1-800-901-0881 with the item's SKU or product ID number and an automated system will tell you what other stores have that same item.

What will you find at Tuesday Morning? A lot! From toys to books to sports equipment to electronics to bedding and linens to home decorations to collectibles to jewelry and more! You can check out some of their offerings online at: www.tuesdaymorning.com. The best deals will be in the stores.

Here are the basics you need to know about Tuesday Morning:

- **Mailing List.** Get on their mailing list *and* on their email list. Sometimes you'll be notified of sales and deals sooner from one source than the other. Sign up for both HERE. (http://www.etreasures.tuesdaymorning.com)
- **Sales Date.** Unlike other stores, their sales are based on items newly in stock. The day of the sale will be the first time you see those items in the store. Their sales used to start at 8:00 a.m. on the chosen Tuesday morning (yep, they named the stores after their preferred sales dates!) but recently they've started them on Sunday morning at 9:00. Read the fine print on the sale flyer/email to be sure.
- **Frequency.** There is generally one sale a month. They will often close the store for a day or two before the sale to stock new items.

- **Rain Checks.** Items are available first-come, first-serve. There are no rain checks or restocking at Tuesday Morning.
- **Discounts over time.** In addition to special sales, items are discounted over time. The longer something is in the store, the more likely you'll find it 20%-40% off the already discounted price.
- **Clearance.** There are clearance shelves in each section with these reduced items. Look for the yellow stickers.
- **Special Sales.** Several times a year there is a special sale where yellow-ticketed items are reduced up to 90%. These offer the very best deals. They'll be announced in the print version of their flyer and usually last for a weekend or until the sale merchandise sells. I've bought things for as low as five cents that I sold later for $15. While there are always items on clearance at Tuesday Morning, for the big sales they'll pull all the stickered items together and offer their deepest discounts of the year.
- **Rewards Program.** Tuesday Morning has just launched its rewards program called Tuesday Morning Perks. You earn rewards by shopping at Tuesday Morning. You also get perks like a longer return period – good news for resellers. You need to sign up in the store.

Long before I started my Amazon business, I was a Tuesday Morning shopper. It may be tempting to buy for yourself rather than for inventory!

Take Action!

1. Set up your Scanfob and smartphone.
2. Have your criteria firmly in mind. You may even want to write down your "buy triggers" on a piece of paper to take with you.
3. Determine your shopping budget.
4. Go shopping.
5. Save your items to ScanPower Mobile so you can access them later.
6. Price, label and ship your items.

13

How To Work A Book Sale

Walking into a book sale can be intimidating – so many books, so little time! Where do you start? This chapter shares my recent experience at a book sale to give you an idea of how I approach a sale.

I am 10 minutes late to the opening day of the book sale. It is like watching piranha feed. The frenzy is on; the noise bounces off the bare walls and industrial ceiling; the volunteers are sparkly and overeager to help me. I fight my way to the back room which is where the non-fiction books are located. It is a madhouse of scanners tripping over each other and their damn carts (note to self: tomorrow bring bags, not boxes. Close quarters). These guys are pros because it is fairly quiet, and the sounds on their scanners are turned off.

I scan the sections and notice there is no one standing by Self-Help and Parenting, two of my favorite sections. I start there. Over the course of about 2.5 hours people pass me or pull out one or two books but no one joins me in systematically scanning the books. I pull out over 100 books and then have to leave for my day job.

By the time I leave, many of the scanners are gone. What the...? Past experience tells me I won't see them again until Sunday, bargain day. This puzzles me but it's part of the reason why I'm not bothered by a lot of scanners at a sale. Last week I pulled out over 400 books from a big, heavily advertised sale, and I was pretty much the only scanner for two of those days. On the final day, I scanned self-help and then parenting, and I was clearly the only scanner that had gone through them. I found many, many books I can sell for $12-$15 at low ranks.

Check out the room – go where others aren't

I got a price sheet at the front and a map (it's a big sale). I looked first to see where the other scanners were – and where I could work without too much hassle.

I considered DVDs, CDs and videos, but left them for Sunday since they are $3-$6 a piece (for books on CD) – a bit rich for my blood today.

Most book sales have a half-off day at the end or a bag/box sale where each bag is $10 that kind of thing, so it is usually worth coming the final day even if you think the books are picked over. Last week I pulled about 150 books during the final hours of the sale.

Know Your Rules

Before you go, be sure to have your rules in mind and stick to them. For example, I'm trying to increase the turnover of my inventory. I have a lot of "long tail" sales in my inventory, so for new purchases I'm keeping my ranking to 1 million or less except for textbooks or books with a very high return.

For books where I'm paying $1, I want to sell them for a minimum of $8. That gives me the return I desire after fees and shipping costs. For the $2 books, I want to see around $9. These are my rules. Yours may be different. On the cheap day, I'll adjust this down. Last week I stuffed enough books in each bag that my cost per book was 30 cents, for example.

Scan Everything

Many non-fiction and textbooks don't have barcodes, which is more work. I scan the ones with barcodes and put the others in a pile. Once I have a big stack, I go through and speak the ISBN#s into ScanPower Mobile. Most scanners don't bother because they care more about speed and volume – and I do that myself sometimes in other categories like business and religion – but textbooks are generally worth my time because they can sell for $25-$75 and more.

ScanPower Mobile Tip – Manual ISBN# Entry

In ScanPower Mobile, you click on the white box at the top (usually it has the ISBN# from the previous book in it) and a keyboard comes up. You can type in the ISBN#. In addition, if you click on the microphone icon, you can speak the number in (on Android and iPhones that have speech capabilities). I find this to be faster than typing in. Occasionally I'll find that there is a space in the number where I paused when speaking the number in. I touch the blank space, delete it and then touch the magnifying glass icon. This brings up the book in ScanPower Mobile.

The only downside of speaking your numbers in is that you'll draw curious people to you. I hand out several business cards at most book sales.

Scan Everything Part II

Last week even though my fellow scanners had already been through the sections I also scanned, such as cookbooks, religion and business, I filled many boxes worth of good items. I made sure to scan the boxes under the tables (remember that pocket chair I recommend? It is a real knee saver), and I checked the textbooks that didn't have barcodes. In addition, I went to the trouble to pick off some bookstore labels. This was part of what baffled me. Borders and Barnes & Noble stickers just slip right off and the other scanners had not bothered to check the barcode underneath? Don't make this mistake! I got several Used-Very Good and Used-Like New books this way!

If your fingernails are paper thin or chewed up, bring a Scotty Peeler – it's worth the few seconds of work.

Why do other sellers leave good books behind? Mostly because they have a different criteria than I do. They may, for example, only be interested in books they can sell for $20 or more. Or perhaps it has to be under 500,000 in rank. You can be confident as you go to your next sale that very few people there will have the same criteria you do, which will offer you opportunities even after others scan a section.

Paperback Books

There are two kinds of paperback books – softcovers and mass market paperbacks. The softcovers are bigger and more like hardback books but with paper covers. They cost more (good for us!) and the barcode on the back is the actual ISBN# which will bring up the book data in ScanPower Mobile.

Mass Market paperback books are smaller with tiny text. The barcode on the back cover is usually NOT the ISBN#. There's a reason for this, but you really don't want to know (publishing is a weird and backward industry). What you DO need to know is that the correct barcode is on the inside front cover. Scan that one and the book should pop right up in ScanPower. If the book is old and there is no interior barcode, you'll need to look up the ISBN# on the book publishing page and type or speak it in. Sometimes on older books the ISBN# is in tiny print on the spine.

Don't Forget Amazon!

It is easy to get excited by a high price under the FBA seller column and to forget to check the Amazon price at the top. There were several 8.5"x11" teacher activity books, etc., that were stapled booklets (for easier copying) that I nearly bought for 25 cents each until I saw the Amazon price of $2.50. Whoops!

Don't Always Compete On Price

For several of the textbooks, the lowest price was ridiculous. Some FBA sellers were taking a loss on their books. I guess they hadn't updated with the new fees yet. The crazy-making part of this was that there was no reason to price their books so low in the first place. They could easily have priced that book for $25+ and not $4.

Based on the rank of the book (it was selling) and the number of units the low-ballers had (1 usually), I sometimes buy those books with the intention of selling them for the higher price. Alternatively, by the time my book gets to the warehouse, there's a good chance their cheap units will be gone and my $25 copy will be the lowest price FBA. Even if it takes a couple of months to sell my book, I'll make good margin on it. I only paid $2 for hardbacks and $1 for paperbacks.

Condition

Some people are nervous about books because there are rules and because they are uncertain about condition. In your contract with Amazon and in the FBA Seller handbook (you can find it in Seller Central), Amazon lays out the rules and guidelines. Be sure to read this!

As a rule of thumb, look at the book and ask yourself, "If I got this in the mail from Amazon, would I think it was new? Like New? Very Good, Good, or Acceptable?" After all, you are a consumer, too! Most books at a book sale are going to fall in the Acceptable to Very Good range, with the majority being Good.

When I'm looking at my scanner and considering how much the book might sell for, I am comparing my condition with the same conditions on Amazon – Used-Very Good to Used-Very Good, that kind of thing.

If the book is a used library book with all those stickers, etc., you cannot list it for any condition better than Good. Library books are Good for the most part, then, unless they are in bad shape with covers all banged up and torn, dog-eared pages, etc. PS. Don't remove the special stickers from library books. You'll ruin the book and you don't have to. Just tell the buyer it is a library book in your notes.

There are several key factors to look at when considering condition:

- **Book cover** – yep, judge the book by its cover. It's a big factor and the number one factor for declaring a book Like New or Very Good.

- **Spine** – is the spine still tight? Maybe the book has only been read once or not at all. Statistically, about 40% of the books bought are never read. They are given as gifts or the buyer thinks he/she will read it, but doesn't. The book ends up at an estate sale or book sale in great shape – although the cover may be showing some shelf wear. A tight spine indicates a better condition and that the book wasn't read.

- **Interior** – highlighting, pencil notes, dog ears – these all need to be noted in your condition notes and they bring the book down in value. If there are just a few pencil marks, you may want to erase them. If the whole book is annotated – then indicate it in your book notes and move on to the next book. Highlights and notes automatically drop a book to Used-Good condition.

- **Signed by the author** – if the book is signed by the author and you are absolutely sure the author signed it because you watched her do it, then you can indicate it in the notes as a way to increase value. However, if you find it in a book sale, you have to tell the buyer that you cannot confirm authenticity. Buyers are very touchy about this. It probably is genuine, but you don't know for sure.

- **Personal inscription** – a few words and a signature is fine, just note it as a personal inscription. If the writer wrote a love letter taking up the whole page, you need to note this in more detail. I've been known to recommend to buyers that they cut that page out of the book if it bothers them.

- **CDs/DVDs** – if the original book had a DVD, CD or software with it, then your version **must** have it as well – no exceptions! Be sure to check. A lot of those ACT/SAT guides and computer books have DVDs.

Think about condition before you buy. Amazon has very specific guidelines. Be sure to read them at this link (requires login to Seller Central): http://bit.ly/BookCondition. Generally, you will get in the most trouble selling something for Good that the buyer thinks was Acceptable, or Very Good that they think is Good, so try to think like a buyer when you are looking at the book.

There are some sellers who won't sell Acceptable copies just because they don't want a return. Ironically, I have the least amount of trouble with Acceptable. Most people understand that Acceptable=crappy and are buying it for the cheap price rather than the pretty cover. Many students use fabric book covers over their textbooks anyway so they only care about the interior.

I will put a book back down if the interior has too many written notes or filled-in answers. Highlights are OK, but notes, answers and other mark-ups are distracting to buyers. I'll flip through at the book sale and check, but sometimes I still get home and find out that a page was ripped out, heavily marked up, etc., and I can't sell it.

Unless the book is shrink-wrapped in plastic and has clearly never been opened, you can't sell it as New. I'm also very careful about Used-Like New. You have a bit more latitude there (very minor shelf wear, tight spine), but if it doesn't look like you just walked out of a book store, I recommend Used-Very Good for those books. You don't know how the book might look after going through the warehouse and sitting on a shelf at Amazon. It is safer to go for Used-Very Good.

Forbidden Fruit: Avoid these headaches

- Rare and collectible books – unless you are an approved collectible book seller by Amazon, you cannot list or sell in this category. If you find a book that you suspect is rare or collectible and the price is right, pick it up and then go find yourself a rare book dealer or an auction house to sell it.

- Advanced reader's copies – it is forbidden to sell these on Amazon unless the book is no longer in print, and then you have to note it in your description that this is an ARC. I accidentally sent about 20-30 in to Amazon and got a stern "fix this now or lose your selling privileges email" from them. Ironically, Amazon caught me so quickly because I DID note it in my book notes! I ended up having Amazon destroy them before any of them sold. Whew!

- Teacher's editions – It is easy to confuse a teacher's edition of a textbook with the student's version. You cannot sell Teacher's editions. Amazon will NOT let you help cheating students this way. You will sometimes see merchant sellers with a teacher's edition of a book. I'm not sure if the rules are different for them, or if they just haven't been caught yet. Regardless, don't make this mistake. It's not worth losing your right to sell on Amazon forever. Sometimes teacher's editions are larger than the student edition, or they say "TE" on the spine. They will definitely note it inside and frequently somewhere on the cover.

What do I buy?

The short answer is: anything that sells. Because there is no way I can scan all the books at a sale, I select categories that are most likely to have good books in them and I prioritize.

<u>Top Tier</u>
- Textbooks – recent editions or rare and interesting collectibles
- Business
- Religion
- Spirituality (often found in Religion) and alternative beliefs
- Crafts/Hobbies – Knitting, Sewing, Gardening – all kinds of "how to"
- Cookbooks (certain ones) – rare, "how-to", and ones that you grew up with
- Self-Help – addiction, incest recovery, overeating, etc.
- Health/Nutrition – NOT diet books. Cancer recovery, ADD, etc.

Second Tier: If I have time
- Reference
- Sports/exercise
- Children's Books – picture books that are in Very Good to Like New condition are best
- Videos – "how-to" and specialty videos not available in DVD format or on Netflix
- CDs/DVDs – Books on CD are good. DVDs should be hard to find or collections like "Taxi: Season One" kind of thing. Most movies are on Netflix and Amazon and the DVDs aren't worth much.

Third Tier
- Classics/literature – bought by college students
- Science Fiction/fantasy
- Murder mystery/thrillers
- Contemporary novels
- Travel – only newer ones. These mostly have a short shelf life as new ones come out annually.
- NO BODICE RIPPERS. Spare yourself the pain and futility.

You'll notice that "fiction" is third tier. It is always my last resort. At a book sale my time is better spent on non-fiction for the most part.

This is my list and my priorities. You may feel differently. I know one seller who specializes in rare and older books. He makes a killing at almost any book sale because he's looking for the books that no one wants and he knows what he's doing.

The important thing is to work the sale as hard and as long as you can and to find out for yourself what categories are most valuable to you.

. . . .

Day two of the book sale. I enter an entire room devoted to textbooks and educational materials. It was swarmed with scanners and shoppers yesterday so I'm not sure if there will be anything left. I decide that if I don't find much in 10 minutes, I'll go to another section. I work the room for about three hours and leave with over 100 books all at ranks under 2 million (my personal outer limit for textbooks since they sell mostly in June, August and January), most well under 1 million. There is no one in this big room with me except the anxious volunteer who keeps checking to make sure I don't need anything. Not one person. This sale has advertised over 100,000 books. I'm in one of the biggest metropolitan areas in the country. Where are my competitors?

. . . .

Day three of the book sale. Today is Saturday. There will be more scanners today and tomorrow, but I'm not worried. One of my students has already cleared out crafts and hobbies so no need to spend time there. That still leaves me tens of thousands of books in nonfiction to plow through.

This is why I don't worry about sharing information or teaching others. There is room and opportunity for many, and very few will work the business the way I do.

While I don't mind other scanners at a sale, the very best sales have NO scanners. I have several like that on my list, and I keep them to myself. Scouting at one of those sales is dazzling. It seems like every other book fits my criteria. I've been known to clear off entire tables at some sales.

For this reason, I strongly suggest you branch out from the free online book sale finders. They generally have the most advertised sales...and the most scouted. Over time as you find untapped sales, add them to your list so you can go again and again. I'm a customer of Frank Florence's paid service (see Resources) and I like it. I have a lot of sales on my list that even Frank doesn't know about, though. There is no substitute for doing your own research in your own neighborhood.

The best sources of book sales are the Friends of the Public Library groups that nearly every library has. They put on the sales and raise money for the library. School districts and universities are also good sources. In addition, charities that collect items for resale often have lots of books. One pet adoption charity I know of gets entire estates in at a time, and it is happy to get rid of books. The more I buy, the better the deal they give me. You want a sale that has lots of donations and not just library books. Generally you will find other items at these sales as well, like toys, CDs, VHS, DVDs and more.

14

AMAZON'S IMPORTANT REPORTS FOR SELLERS

By this point, your first shipment is on its way to the Amazon warehouse and you are probably wondering, "What's next?" The next thing to do is to familiarize yourself with Seller Central.

When your shipment reaches the warehouse, you will get a couple of emails from Amazon. The first will tell you it is in the warehouse. The second will tell you when your shipment has been processed and your listings are live.

That's when the fun begins. Assuming you had fast-selling items, you should see sales within the first week. I had my first sale within a few hours of my listings going live.

Now that you have sales, all those wonderful reports Amazon provides become relevant. The most important one is about the money, of course!

Go to the "Payments" report, which you'll find under "Reports" in the main navigational bar at the top of the page. As you will see, this covers the current two-week payment period. You can access previous payments under the dropdown menu.

This is a summary page. You can click on "Transactions" from this page to see all the transactions that make up this report. This is particularly helpful as you are coming up to speed on Amazon's fees. I broke out those fees earlier in this book, but they are hard to understand until you see them in action here on your Payments report. Transactions include everything from shipping via UPS to refunds (it happens to everyone) to commissions. All you need to do is subtract your inventory acquisition and shipping supply expenses from this number.

Selling on Amazon is a bit like buying and selling real estate. Your money is made at the time of the deal. Don't take a bad deal and hope it will get better later. If you make wise choices with your purchases and build in a cushion for price fluctuations, refunds and other expenses, you'll do well.

By the way, the Refunds on this page are not necessarily buyer refunds. Amazon uses this section to charge and then refund you money for Prime buyers using expedited shipping. It is to your benefit, but the accounting can be confusing when you look at it the first time.

As you sell inventory, be sure to run the other reports Amazon gives you and learn how they can help you. Most of them are Excel files that you download to your computer.

The other pages where you will spend a lot of time are your inventory pages.

On the inventory page you can see how many MSKUs you have used with Amazon. You can sort the information on this page by the hyperlinked categories at the top of the chart – MSKU, Product Name, Date Created and Price.

On this page, you can change your prices manually and they will take effect immediately. You can also search your inventory by title, SKU, ISBN and ASIN. The Low Price indicator is not particularly helpful to me since I am rarely the lowest-priced seller: still, when I am, it shows that with a green checkmark.

Now let's go to the "Inventory Amazon Fulfills." While the previous report covered all inventory, this report is only for FBA merchandise. If you sell both self-fulfilled and Amazon-fulfilled, you'll look at the first report to see everything. For me, this report is the same as my "All Inventory" report because I only sell FBA.

On this page, I have greater search capabilities. I can also search for items and perform bulk activities like "Send/Replenish Inventory" and others. I can download this report as a comma-delimited file, which opens in Excel, where, I can perform more strategic data sorts.

I can also change prices on this page manually. I can sort this page by "Fulfillable" which shows me the items where I have the most units first. I check these pretty regularly.

If you see an item with the word Reserved on the side, it means that one has just sold, but not yet shipped. Buyers have a window of time to change their mind and that's why there's a Reserved.

If you click the "Show ASIN/FNSKU" box at the top of the page, the listings will show you the ASIN number. You can click on that to see the product on that page and check prices. If you decide you want to change your price, come back to this page, change the price, click the square box to the far left of the item, and then click "Submit Prices" at the top of the page. You can change as many prices as you like on this page before clicking "Submit Prices," but be sure to do it before going to the next page or your changes will not be saved.

Next, the "Unit Volume" in the last column shows you the measurements Amazon uses to calculate your storage fees. If you are ever curious as to which items are taking up the most amount of space, click here.

Lastly, there is one more important piece of information: how to get help. Amazon has wonderful seller support. You can get a live person on the phone and he or she will work with you until the problem is resolved. The Help link is at the top of every page.

TAKE ACTION!

1. Become familiar with the many reports Amazon gives you.
2. Check your inventory and payment reports frequently.
3. Sort your sales each month so you know which ones are subject to sales tax. Download the spreadsheet each month for your records.
4. Learn the simple way to reprice through the "Inventory Amazon Fulfills" page.

15

They Did It!

As I mentioned in the beginning, I wrote this book because people kept asking me what I was doing and the PowerPoint presentation I created wasn't enough. The following five people started Amazon FBA businesses over the past year and all of them have realized success. I am grateful to them for sharing their experiences and triumphs. I have learned so much from them in the process. Here are some of the lessons learned:

Discontinued Toy Is Online Gold

My Dad has become an avid consumer of BigLots and Toys "R" Us ads and coupons. He shops there regularly and gets good deals. One day he found a deal he couldn't believe was real when it popped up on his phone. He found a particular X-Box guitar controller that was selling "buy two, get one free" for $4.50 each.

For $9.00, he bought three and sent them in to Amazon priced at $65.00 each. They sold immediately. Then he ran out and bought as many more as he could find. Every time Toys "R" Us re-stocked, he bought them all.

He called me to tell me about it and I looked all over my local Toys "R" Us store. When I asked for help, I was told the product was discontinued and no longer for sale in their stores or online. Happily, for Dad, they were restocked several times in his store in Wilmington, North Carolina.

My Dad is a great example of someone for whom this business works part-time. He's the busiest retired guy you'll ever meet with board meetings, local politics, tennis matches and church responsibilities. This business allows him to make extra income in his own time and way. He is able to take advantage of the two-hour and one-day sales that often occur in the middle of a week. Before starting this business, he knew nothing about toys. Now he knows what's important – people will pay for what they want and just because it doesn't make sense to him, doesn't mean he can't sell it.

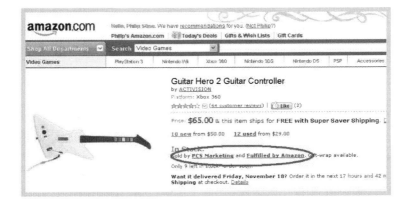

CHOOSY MOMS DRIVE THE BABY MARKET

On my first BigLots shopping trip, Chris Green taught me a lot about the concept of "anything with a barcode." While toys made perfect sense to me, I hadn't thought about baby items (or many of the other categories for that matter). Chris found a particular brand of baby wipes for under $2 that were selling online for $25.

My eyes goggled. Twenty-five dollars for butt wipes? When diapers and wipes are sold in practically every store? As a parent of young kids himself, Chris spoke authoritatively when he said, "If your kid likes a particular brand of anything, you'll buy it." They did have a nice smell. They were probably discontinued, according to Chris. He bought out the store's stock and sold them all online. A few months later I found some more and sold them, too. Since my happy experience with butt wipes, I've sold adult diapers, too.

As another example of how choosy (mostly) moms drive the baby market, a friend of mine in the business, John, found large quantities of a particular brand of pacifier that was discontinued. He was the only FBA seller. He couldn't believe the markup and hit every store within driving distance. At the peak of his pacifier sales, he was selling over 100 units a week. He's sold baby bottles, nipples (just talking about this with him made me giggle), spoons and baby toys. John doesn't even have children, but he sells to choosy moms.

I sold hundreds of baby spoons in my first year. I bought them for $3 or less at BigLots and other stores, and then I sold them for $10-$15 each. I love baby spoons. They are cheap, lightweight, sell fast and have a great margin. Who on earth would pay so much for a set of plastic spoons? My busy and impatient customers, that's who.

I have sold designer diaper bags, foam booster seats, training potty seats, mobiles, sippy cups, toys, breast milk accessories and much, much more.

BE WILLING TO GET DIRTY

One of the best strategies for this business is to be where others are not. If everyone is sending in the latest gadget from BigLots, you need to be somewhere else. I love BigLots but sometimes the competition with other FBA sellers can be annoying – particularly when some of them participate in a race to the bottom that drives all the prices down.

My friend Lesley spotted a diamond in the rough at a thrift store in a more industrial part of town. When she walked in, the place was dirty, crowded, chaotic, loud and cluttered. Still, she gamely headed over to the bookshelves where she discovered that on Saturdays from 10 a.m. to 2 p.m., all the hardbacks were 20 cents and all the paperbacks were 10 cents.

For less than $10, she left with hundreds of dollars' worth of books. She couldn't even go through them all in one session. When she came back again, she discovered that a lot of fresh (if dusty) inventory was on the shelves, and she left again with hundreds of dollars' worth of books for less than $10. When she took me, it went faster working as a team. We were able to look at video games (25 cents), videos (10 cents) and much, much more. We were completely filthy by the end of day and jubilant as we divvied up our finds. We go back there as often as we can.

INCOMPATIBLE BUSINESS MODELS CAN BE COMPLEMENTARY

I'm a big believer in "co-opetition" where you work together with selected competitors to help everyone succeed. Obviously you have to find the right partners, and it is important to understand what each person wants – it will not be the same for everyone, even though we all want to make money. Sometimes someone with an incompatible business model is a perfect fit.

Super sleuth Lesley found a Craigslist ad where an Amazon merchant seller was offering his rejects for $3 a box. When she checked out his warehouse, she learned that he had over 500,000 books for sale on Amazon on his shelves and thousands of boxes of New, Like New and Very Good books that didn't fit his profile. She took a few boxes to start and discovered that the merchant's team did not scan books without a barcode, which gave her some fantastic finds with older books. In addition, quite a few of the books that did not fit the merchant's model fit hers as an FBA seller. The ones that didn't work for her, she donated to her local library and charities. Most of them were blockbusters that will do very well with the reading public.

I went back with her on one trip and bought 65 boxes (all my garage could store at the time). Boy was I tired that day. I made my way through them in between more urgent shipments. It took about a year. I cleared around $120 a box on average after expenses – well worth the $3 a box investment!

RETHINK STORES THAT ARE REMODELING

I was annoyed when my local grocery store remodeled. Nothing was in its regular place and the store was chaotic. It took twice as long to shop. What I didn't realize at first was how many non-food items are for sale at a grocery store. As part of its remodel, the store was clearing out its shelves at deeply discounted prices. I brought in my scanner and found all kinds of bargains both for my family and to sell online.

While we can sell food online FBA, I hadn't started at the time of the remodel. Much of the food that was on sale was getting close to its expiration date, which was fine for us to eat, but I wouldn't have been able to send it to Amazon. Instead, I found kitchen gadgets, toys, games and small appliances on sale that were fine for FBA.

On another day, I stepped inside an office supply store that was undergoing major renovations. They had a big banner up outside that said, "We're Open!" underneath the scaffolding. I came to buy some stickers and left with over $1,000 worth of computer games, software and manuals. The brand-new games were $1 each and I sold them for $12-$20. There were over 20 copies of the LabelFactory Deluxe software at $5 each and I sold them all for $45 each. I bought an old version of Microsoft FrontPage for $25 and sold it within two weeks for $252.99.

Now I look for stores that are remodeling. I found another office supply store recently that was remodeling. I bought 35 software packages for $5 each and eight iPad cases for $5 each. With one exception, all are selling at $20 and up. I'm expecting to clear around $600 after expenses and I spent about 20 minutes in the store — that's a good return on investment even when you add in the hour or two. I'll spend removing price stickers, labeling and shipping to Amazon.

What Were They Thinking?

Some stores buy popular merchandise for all the wrong reasons. When a customer enters the door, they usually have a specific idea of what they want and why they think they'll find it at that particular retail outlet. If they find something outside of that expectation – even if it is something they might gladly buy in another environment – they leave it alone.

I went into a Blockbuster one day to rent a video and was surprised to see a big clearance table with vacuum cleaners, wall stickers, plush toys, books and an assortment of other bewilderments. They were at a deep discount and I bought most of them. The vacuum cleaners sold so fast, they hardly spent any time at all in the warehouse. I profited from that experience and now I keep an eye out for stores selling items that are weird for their category. There is a good chance that item will be on sale later.

Other stores stock up seasonally on merchandise, like toys and games that they don't sell year-round. They may offer discounts before, during and after the season. For this reason, I keep an eye open at Home Depot, Lowe's and my local grocery store right after Christmas for steep discounts. Toys sell all year on Amazon.

I bought Toy Story 3 games last year at Aldi's grocery in my neighborhood for $19.99 and listed them for $50.

Just Do It!

My friend Lynn started her business November, 2011 and realized incredible success with holiday sales. She has great intuition for what will be popular and made some super toy buys (and sales!) before a lot of other FBA Sellers caught on to how hot they were. She taught me about Inkoos and together we bought out our local Targets in Dallas and Chicago. She proved to me that there were deals to be found at Target – I never seriously scouted there before she told me what she found – and Wal-Mart.

She immediately understood margin and that an OK deal was really a bad deal because it took money and attention away from the next really good deal. She quickly realized there were more deals than she could possibly buy and so she picks and chooses. She got a Target credit card while standing in the checkout line. She not only got bonus savings for signing up that day, she now saves 5% on all her purchases until she reaches her limit each month. As long as you pay off the card quickly, it is a great deal. If you carry a balance, the rate is around 22% - steep.

She follows the 3X rule. As a busy mom and teacher, she does not have time for any activity or purchase that isn't going to be productive. One of her personal rules is that she won't buy anything too big to fit in one of her box sizes (18"x12"x12" or 20"x20"x20") because it is too much time and hassle – even with a big payout. She would rather buy and sell three or four smaller items and get the same profit, than to have to find a special box size, call UPS to pick it up, etc., for an oversized item. This is her rule. Once I sold my first slow cooker for $71, I bought a bunch of bigger boxes. You will have your own rules.

Lynn test-drove this book and made it much better with her feedback. She got her business up and running in a week, and she is selling more than I am in my second holiday season. She had me to answer her questions, which helped speed the process, but all the work was hers and she is reaping the rewards. Her second check from Amazon was over $7,500!

With my friend Lesley, I told her about FBA and before I even knew how interested she was, she had started her business – and her brother, too. She discovered the huge warehouse where we can buy books for $3 a box and the thrift store that sells books for 10 cents on Saturdays. Lesley is also the one that told me about an unbelievable one-day sale at Tuesday Morning one weekend. I'll make about $4K off the inventory I bought in a few hours. I learn as much from Lesley as she ever did from me about this business.

My friend John took about two-three weeks to get everything set up, and he had trouble with the technology (he is also a Mac user so I could not help him), but once he was functioning, he is selling like crazy. He gives me great tips on baby items.

My dad took several months before he started sending in large shipments. He started with his books and media, and he made small experiments. Once he felt ready, he was like a house on fire. He calls me from Toys "R" Us with exciting finds, and it tickles me. He was the first one to find the slow cookers at BigLots and to encourage me to try a new category. Since then I've sold coffee makers, food processors and pressure cookers as well.

The common thread with all these stories is that they took the plunge and tried it. Each person's business is uniquely their own. The time they put into their businesses, the investment in inventory and the size of their businesses is a reflection of their personal values, resources and decisions – as yours will be – but they are all successful and happy that they started.

16

You Can Do It, Too!

You've come all this way and read the whole book. Hopefully, you are here because you have a shipment on its way to Amazon and thought you'd check in to see if I had anything else to say! I do, but not in this book. I write a lot on my blog at www.sellstepbystep.com and I hope to see you there or on Facebook: www.facebook.com/MakeThousandsonAmazon.

If you've not yet taken action, now is the time. Make a commitment to yourself that you'll have at least one box on its way to Amazon by this time next week. The first sale – when you know for sure this business is going to work – is such a rush! And selling never gets old. I'm still thrilled every time I get an email telling me that something has sold.

It's a cliché, but if I can do it, you can too. I'm a wife and a mom trying to help my family make ends meet. What is remarkable about my story is that I can operate this business on such a small scale and be successful. It truly is a manageable part-time business. Now that you know how I do it, you can too. I have good tools to maximize my time and make me a smarter buyer, and I have a good partner in Amazon to help me reach the largest retail audience in the world and to meet their buying expectations.

This is not a risk-free business, but it is a risk-manageable business. The cost of entry is low and the rewards are high. I look forward to seeing you succeed online and would love to hear your fun stories of things that you can't believe sold, deals so good you felt guilty, and the joy of selling online overall.

Cheers,

http://www.sellstepbystep.com

17

DON'T MAKE MY MISTAKES!

Over the past few years, I've made mistakes and learned a lot from them. You'll make mistakes, too, but hopefully you can make new mistakes instead of these!

1. Check the video/DVD/CD inside the case before you buy used media. Sometimes the case will not match the contents and you'll return home with junk instead of jewels.

2. Make sure the tape or disc is in good condition. Apply scratch filler if need be or don't buy it if you are not sure. Returns for poor product quality hurt your rating as a seller.

3. Don't sell a video, DVD or CD in Used-Acceptable condition. It is not worth creating an unhappy customer. Books are OK in Used-Acceptable condition – just be sure to let them know what they're getting up front.

4. Beware of sets! I bought a bunch of Tae Bo videos not realizing that the prices I saw on the scanner were for the set, not individual tapes. This happens a lot with workout videos, food, diapers and some office supplies. Because I don't have a complete set – and have not been able to find the missing tape – the videos are gathering dust on my bookshelf.

5. Beware of different items with the same ISBN. This happens when there is an assortment or an item typically sells by the case. Pacifiers, diapers, medical supplies and items that sell in different colors should be checked more closely when you scan. I've learned to surf out to Amazon on my phone when something seems "too good to be true" or when the picture for a pink item and a blue item come up with the same image. If a customer thinks she is buying a pink pacifier, it can't be blue.

6. Don't price the same or higher than Amazon! More than once I've gotten home and discovered that I was so excited by the other FBA prices (nice and high) that I didn't see that Amazon was selling the product New for less. I once returned 20 videos to BigLots because I didn't notice this. We call this the "walk of shame" in the business.

7. Don't sell calendars in January! You can sell calendars year round (I sold a 2011 calendar in

September of the same year), but after the first week in January – watch out! That's when Amazon slashes all its calendar prices to the bone. In January, I had about 30 calendars left in inventory. Some that Amazon was selling below my cost; I decided to leave up there and see what happened. Others I dropped in price and cleared out. I've been surprised, but I've continued to sell a calendar or two every month and I only have five left in inventory. This year I will sell out before January.

8. **Print off, read and reread your contract with Amazon!** It is horribly long but it includes very important issues to which you've agreed. For example, you cannot sell advanced reader's copy or promotional use only items in books, music or other media. I sent in a bunch (I'm in the publishing business and had a ton in my personal library) and got a warning from Amazon. I ended up having Amazon destroy them for me. They are quite serious about this issue. Another example is that library books – no matter how nice – cannot list for better than Used-Good condition and you have to disclose that it is a library book.

9. Amazon is also very particular about how you ship boxes to them. No foam peanuts, no newspaper. Check all the fine print or be unpleasantly surprised later. All items that have plush or cloth exposed must be covered in a plastic bag or shrink-wrapped

so they don't get dirty in the warehouse. This has recently been expanded to include toys – plush or not – that are exposed in any way. If you use bags, be sure to create safety warning labels and put one on each bag: You can also buy them on Amazon. I printed my own for a long time until I bought bags that already had the warning printed on them:

WARNING! Keep away from small children. The thin film may cling to nose and mouth and prevent breathing.

10. Tell Amazon that something is a set. I have stickers that say, "THIS IS A SET – DO NOT SEPARATE." I made the mistake once of not doing that and it was a mess because they opened the box and of course nothing inside was labeled. Sigh. Ultimately it was all fixed.

11. Put the expiration date on food. Amazon requires this in large font. I have stickers that say "BEST BY: ____/_____/_____" in the largest possible font that will print on my label. I use a black Sharpie to write in the expiration date. No expiration date and they could just throw your food out or charge you for creating a sticker themselves.

12. Some toys have food in them. I was selling a young chef cooking kit with pans and other cooking

accessories. It also had food packets. Some of my kits took a year to sell (they sell fast at Xmas, slow the rest of the year) and I got an angry Mom upset about the expired food packets inside. I gave her a partial refund and an apologetic letter which made her happy again. I was thinking "toy" but it was also food. I didn't get in trouble with Amazon because it was sold in the toy category, but I made a customer unhappy.

13. Keep an eye on your inventory and pricing. Amazon lowers its prices without warning. Sometimes it is a short one-day (all mysteries 15% off!) or one-week sale. Sometimes it is just a price cut to compete with its FBA sellers and/or clear out overstocked inventory. If you have many units of the item in question, be sure to check it manually and don't rely solely on your repricer. If it is an Amazon sale and not a permanent price cut, you may want to wait for the price to go back up.

14. Review your sales every day. I just about ripped my hair out when I realized that I had made a typo – a HUGE one – in the price of a coffeemaker I was selling. Instead of around $80, I sold it to someone for $3.99. It hurt like heck to take a loss like that (It cost me around $20 to buy it), but at least I caught it and fixed it before most of my others sold.

15. Read your feedback regularly. I was slammed with three unhappy customers on the same day, which had never happened before. My rating dropped below 90%, which is awful. I have so far resolved the issues with two of them such that they have removed their negative feedback and my rating has gone back up to 97%.

18

RESOURCES

GET HELP!

Throughout your selling career there will come times when you need help. I call Amazon all the time with questions. They are my business' best friend. I have a detailed blog post about getting help of all kinds from the vendors, from Amazon, etc. I've re-posted it in my members-only area for you. Below I've listed how to get help from Amazon, but be sure to check out the blog or membership area if you need more than that.

Amazon "Contact Us"

This is my go-to resource for a lot of problems. Inside your SellerCentral, click on the "Help" link. From there look for "Contact Us" in the middle right-hand-side of the page and click on it. You will now have a huge variety of problems to choose from. Click on the one that best covers your issue and fill in as much information as possible about your issue including MSKU, ASIN and any other relevant facts. At the very bottom of the email page you will be given the option to either email your issue to Amazon or have them call you. I usually have them call me. Type in your phone number, click call and your phone will ring right away.

At first you will get a general seller customer service person. Depending on your issue, they may pass you on to an FBA specialist. They can see everything you wrote in that email form which saves time on the call and can cut-and-paste the ASIN and MSKU, etc., which is why it is worthwhile to fill out the form rather than just drop down to the "call me" line. The FBA support team is absolutely wonderful. They will sit on the phone with you until your problem is solved. I've learned so much from them.

You can, of course, send an email. That option is most likely to be outsourced to someone overseas. They are very fast on response, but everything is pretty much auto-scripted if you know what I mean. Email is great for issues where you know what the problem is already and you are simply giving directions "Please expedite HazMat approval on ASIN#..." Or "Please remove this negative feedback." In fact, for negative feedback they insist you use email and not call.

Be sure you are contacting customer service from inside your SellerCentral and not your personal buyer account. I had a reader do that once. He was really frustrated because no one could help him. It turned out he was talking to the wrong people inside of Amazon.

HELPFUL BOOKS

You can find the most up-to-date list of recommended books on my blog at: http://www.sellstepbystep.com. I'm constantly learning from other sellers in this business, which makes me a better and better seller.

Amazon – *The Quick and Dirty Guide* and ***Leftover Gold I & II*** and ***Retail Flipping*** – Steve Lindhorst http://mcsurf.us/1447LFE and http://mcsurf.us/19ziqOk. These books gave me good ideas for sourcing inventory from garage sales to estate sales, warehouse sales, auctions and much more. Steve gives many examples of finding treasure where other people only saw junk. He also taught me how to make sure my products were worthy of sale on Amazon. He talks about cleaning up books, DVDs and CDs. His *Retail Flipping* book focuses on when the best time is to buy certain items for the best price. He includes a month-by-month calendar of what to buy when. I highly recommend this book.

Creative Sourcing for Booksellers – Frank Aaron Florence. While this book is focused primarily on books, I got several good ideas for places to find cheap inventory. What I've discovered is that there are often cheap DVDs, CDs, software and computer games at the same places where you find books. He has recently updated his book and you can find it on Amazon.com.

Liquidation Gold: A guide for Amazon sellers – by Jessica Larrew. Jessica has built her business up to the point that both she and her husband were able to quit their jobs and now work this business full-time. She has a blog and this book. She sells mostly food and health & beauty. I've learned a ton from her. *Liquidation Gold* teaches you how to locate surplus grocery stores and find amazing deals to sell on Amazon. I wrote about my experience putting her book in practice on my blog. You can also find a link to her book there.

Retail Arbitrage: The Blueprint for Buying Retail Products to Sell Online for Big Profits – Chris Green's book is a must-have. http://amazon.com/author/chris. Here is a guy who is passionate about selling online and who is a leading seller on Amazon. His advice on pricing and acquiring inventory is invaluable. He is very analytical and clear about how the numbers, not intuition, drive his buying strategies. Now that you have a basic understanding of Amazon's FBA program and ScanPower, his book will help you go to the next level with your business. He's one of the most down-to-earth people I've ever met, and he's genuinely motivated to help people succeed as online sellers.

Selling on Amazon's FBA Program—by Nathan Holmquist; the book that got me started. He very clearly explains how to sell a penny book for $4 on Amazon with FBA. He is now offering the book free at:http://www.sellfba.com/cs.html. I paid close to $30 and thought it was well worth it. It is outdated now, but there's good information in there. His blog is also very interesting. He shares his approach to buying and selling books (primarily) on Amazon.com. www.sellfba.com.

Sell Used Books on eBay, Amazon.com and the Internet for Profit– Skip McGrath's book is very helpful for people who want to sell on multiple platforms including eBay, Half.com, Abe Books and others. http://www.skipmcgrath.com/products/sell-used-books-ebay-amazon.php

The Home-Based Bookstore: Start Your Own Business Selling Used Books on Amazon, eBay or Your Own Web Site – Steve Weber:. Steve's written several books including his most recent, ***Barcode Booty: How I Found and Sold $2 Million of "Junk" on eBay & Amazon and You Can, Too, Using Your Phone***. When I read **Home-Based**, I felt inspired. He made the business seem very accessible. He focused on book selling but has now expanded since he started using ScanPower Mobile. He interviews other sellers in **Booty,** which I found interesting. [Full disclosure: he mentions me as an example in the book on p.22.] He is a multi-platform seller, which I plan to be down the road. He lists a number of online sites where you can buy inventory at a good price. I've been checking them out over time. www.fatwallet.com has captured my interest lately – there are many other sites to investigate.

Legal & Financial Books

Incorporate and Grow Rich – This book helped me understand the benefits of incorporating and taught me how to apply them to my business. Over the years, with the help of my CPA, I've easily saved more than $100,000 in taxes because I'm willing to record things and structure my businesses for maximum tax advantage. It is a bit outdated but the concepts and approach are very helpful. According to Amazon reviewers, this particular edition is disorganized and needed an editor. This was not true of my (much older) version. It was said that a lot of the information is on the company's website which didn't even exist when I first bought the book, so you may want to go to the website first. The reason I liked it so much was it was the first tax book I'd ever read that was written in plain English. You'll want to work with your CPA to understand what the IRS allows today. http://bit.ly/IncAndGrowRich.

Introduction to Sales Tax for Amazon FBA Sellers: Information and Tips to Help FBA Sellers Understand Tax Law (Volume 1) – by Kat Simpson and Michael Rice. Rice is an attorney, Simpson a well-known online seller (both FBA and eBay). The only book specifically written for FBA sellers, it explains a "nexus" and how that concept affects Amazon and, by extension, us. Basically, now that Amazon is falling in line and starting to pay states sales tax, it will only be a matter of time before the states come after small fry like us. My advice to new sellers is don't get distracted right now. There is so much up in the air about this topic at the moment including legislation in congress that could change things. Promise yourself you will look at the sales tax issue down the road after you are confident in your business and making money. After all, you can't pay taxes if you don't make money. http://bit.ly/SaleTax

Start Your Own Corporation: Why the Rich Own Their Own Companies and Everyone Else Works for Them (Rich Dad Advisors). This book is written by an attorney rather than a CPA, and it is focused on asset protection as well as tax reduction. It is a very good book and well written for humans (as compared to lawyers and CPAs!) with lots of helpful examples and relevant case studies.http://bit.ly/GarrettSuttonIncBook. When you finish the book, you'll want to incorporate, believe me. A lot of people avoid incorporating because they think it is expensive, but it actually allows you to save a lot of money legally.

I have additional resources on my blog under the "Helpful Websites, Groups and Bloggers" tab:

SmallBiz CEOs—A great audio resource to help you with the business questions (not Amazon-specific) that come up when you are building your business. The monthly audio newsletter is produced by one of my favorite business consultants since the mid-90s, David Shepherd. The first month is free and it is easy to unsubscribe if it doesn't help you (which is refreshing). You can download the audio newsletter to your phone or however you listen to podcasts on the go. http://bit.ly/DavidShepherdAudio

FBA Forum -- http://bit.ly/fbaforum is a Yahoo group for FBA sellers. There are over 1400 members and the forum is very active. This is a helpful group where newcomers can get advice from more experienced sellers and seasoned sellers can learn new things to grow their businesses. The archives will hold the answers to many of your questions. It is a closed and monitored/facilitated group. You need to be accepted first. Bob Wiley keeps the group focused on FBA-related issues.

ScanPower – www.scanpower.com. There is a lot of information on this site. There is even a "how-to" video showing how you can scan and read your ScanPower Mobile one-handed. Chris is a machine when he is scanning.

Nathan Holmquist – *Book to the Future* is the name of his blog, www.booktothefuture.com

Skip McGrath – a veteran of online sales. He started with eBay and now sells on multiple platforms. http://www.skipmcgrath.com/newsletters/current.shtml. He has a blog and books.

Book Sale Locators

I use all of these resources regularly to help me keep track of book sales in my area and around the country (when I travel). Anything new I find will be posted at: http://www.fbastepbystep.com/book-sale-locators/

Book Sale Finder – this free online service is a billboard of many book sales across the country. The sale hosts (usually libraries) list their sales. While it is not comprehensive, it is very helpful. Most of the mega-sales of 50,000+ books use Book Sale Finder. www.booksalefinder.com

Book Sale Manager – this free service includes upcoming sales and offers the additional tool of organizing your book sales, placing them in Outlook or Gmail for you, and sending reminders of the ones you've chosen. It will even download location information to your GPS device. www.booksalemanager.com

Book Sales Found – This is a paid service by Frank Florence that provides a shortcut to finding book sales in your area. What his team does is compile a database of book sales in your area where there isn't a lot of competition, (i.e. not the cattle calls) and provides you with maps and information. You can even get custom research. Follow this link and you will get a 7-day free trial and the book. After 7-days, it costs $9.99 a month to continue. http://bit.ly/FREEtrialFrank

SUPPLIES

I have a page on my blog, Supplies for your FBA Business, that I keep updated with supplies for your business. It shows pictures and provides links. Because prices change so often, I suggest that when you click through to Amazon (or wherever the link goes) for an item (like the Dymo printer or labels) that you check to see if there is now a cheaper alternative.

I also have my coupon for Scanfob on this page.

ONLINE DEALS

There are many sites, including your favorite retailers, where you can scout for deals. I've tried some purchases from Toys "R" Us and was not impressed— the toys looked beat to death, not cool, inside their boxes. But I've scouted out some items online at other stores that has worked out pretty well like Wal-Mart and Target. If you can combine a good deal with free shipping, you get an extra bonus of a free shipping box. Some sites have coupons, point systems, cash-back...you get the idea. I find scouting online much slower than in the store. If you live far away from stores, online scouting for deals may be very appealing for you. This list is not comprehensive:

BigLots – www.biglots.com. They have regular sales and will notify you in advance if you are a Club member. They also have a **wholesale warehouse**, if you have a sales tax ID, where the prices are terrific and the bulk purchase requirements are not too onerous ($500 minimum order + 15% shipping cost).

Overstock – www.overstock.com. Just like it sounds, this site sells manufacturers' overstocks. Be careful that you are not buying a refurbished product or a second unless the item is for sale on Amazon as a refurbish. You want new-in-box.

Toys "R" Us – www.toysrus.com and www.babiesrus.com. I'm not impressed with the quality of products in their warehouse so it has kept me from shopping with them very much. There are online-only sales, coupons and special store deals that you can only find out about online.

Fat Wallet – www.fatwallet.com. This site consolidates deals from all over the internet and keeps a database of Black Friday deals as they are leaked. As of this writing in October, they have already posted the Black Friday deals for several retailers.

Woot! – www.woot.com. Woot is fun just for its product descriptions. They have super deals, but you can't order more than 3 at a time. However, if your spouse orders 3, you order 3, your kid orders 3...you can still get quite a few. They have one deal a day, and it goes out right after midnight. Once their stock sells out, it's over. Besides regular Woot, they have one for kid products, t-shirts (highly addictive) and wine. You can read my blog post about Woot! on my blog or in the membership site.

eBay – www.ebay.com. Colleagues of mine have scooped up terrific bargains on eBay to resell on Amazon. eBay allows you to set up searches and notifications such that you can be notified if an auction of interest to you is closing. If there aren't other bidders, you can walk away with an amazing bargain. Sometimes an inexperienced seller will make a mistake in the listing that will keep potential buyers away (a misspelling in the title, for example).

Amazon – www.amazon.com. Not to miss the obvious! There are many Amazon sellers who are also inexperienced and who sell products for ridiculously low prices. This is usually because they don't understand their repricer or they don't understand the FBA program. Suddenly a $20 book is selling for 1 penny from an FBA seller. Should you buy it? Of course! It will show up at your door in 2 days for only 1 penny to you (assuming you are an Amazon Prime member).

19

7-STEP BUSINESS STARTER CHECKLIST RECAP

1. **Plan**
   - Decide how much money you can spend on supplies and inventory to start.
   - Determine how much you need to make in order for this to be worthwhile.
   - Decide the name of your business.
   - Will you incorporate or just use a DBA to start? (DBA=Doing Business As).
   - You do not need to decide now if you want to incorporate, but make a note to yourself to think about it later. You may want to read the *Incorporate. and Grow Rich* book listed in the Resources chapter at the end of the book.

2. **Set up your business**
   - Get your desired DBA from your state. Texas has an online database you can search to be sure the business name you

want is available; then you pay a small fee to own it for 10 years.

- Go online to www.irs.gov and request a business tax ID number in the name of your DBA or corporation. Your business does not have to be incorporated to get this number. You can even get one in your name although this is not recommended.
- File for your state sales tax number (you can do it online in most states) so you can buy merchandise tax-free. You can wait to do this until later if you want.
- Open a separate checking account for your business. It does not have to be a business checking account per se, but needs to be separate from your personal account(s) for tax purposes and for ease of accounting. Many banks (like Chase), allow you to set up accounts online.
- Sign up for a UPS business account online using your business tax ID and DBA. Go to http://www.ups.com and click on "New User" to get started.
- Review Amazon's latest fees and set up a spreadsheet to help you determine your break-even point and minimum selling prices.

3. **Order supplies.** Depending on your beginning resources, order/source these supplies. The first four are critical to start. See my website's "Supplies For Your FBA Business" page for specifics on where to get these items.

- USB handheld scanner that plugs into a USB port on your computer.
- Shipping boxes (18"x12"x12" or smaller work well for books). They don't have to be new, but they must be sturdy.
- Packing tape and paper (or bubble wrap or air pillows – NO foam peanuts).
- Free UPS shipping labels (two per 8.5"x11" page). You need to sign up and then wait about 3-4 days until you can place your first order. In the short term you can use regular paper in your printer for your boxes, but you'll like the shipping labels a lot better.
- Dymo LabelWriter 450 Turbo printer (or a Zebra printer). If you already have a printer capable of printing rolls of adhesive labels up to 2"x3" in size, that is worth testing with ScanPower. Dymo and Zebra are the two that I know work for sure. For the short-term, Amazon will print off labels for you on those sheets of labels (Avery 5160 is one) you put in your laser printer.
- Address-sized labels for your Dymo printer (they can range from 1"x2" to 2"x3" in size).

I buy "Dymo Compatible" rather than Dymo brand. They are cheaper.

- Smartphone (ScanPower Mobile runs on phones with the Android operating system and Apple iPhone phones). Amazon.com sells cell phones as low as one penny with a two-year contract. Be sure to check that out if you need a smartphone. For a while, Virgin was offering terrific prices on Android monthly subscription fees – around $40 a month – so be sure to shop around.
- Scanfob Bluetooth™ scanner to use with your smartphone. You don't need this to get started but it will speed up your scouting for inventory by a lot.
- Protective carrier for your Smartphone. (I use an armband/wristband).
- Shipping scale that calculates weights up to at least 75 lbs. I started with my bathroom scale, but a real shipping scale is a lot easier to use.
- Back-up battery for your smartphone and Scanfob. See the one I suggest on my website.

4. **Round up your inventory from around the house**
- Books
- DVDs
- CDs

- Video games
- VHS tapes
- Software with packaging in good shape
- Anything new, still sealed in its original packaging
- Old games with all their pieces (you can sell collectible/discontinued toys on Amazon – but not Used)
- Like-New appliances or household gadgets still in their original box.

5. **Set up your Amazon seller account and ScanPower**
   - See http://www.makethousandsupdates.com for most current links and instructions.
   - Scan, price and label your items.
   - "Ship" your items from ScanPower to Amazon Seller Central™.

6. **Send in your first shipment**
   - Use Amazon's "Seller Central" and 7-step "Shipping Queue" shipment process to prepare your boxes.
   - Pack and weigh your box(es).
   - Take your box(es) to a UPS drop site or arrange a pick-up.

7. **Go shopping for more inventory**
   - Set up your Scanfob and Smartphone.

- Determine the locations of your local BigLots, Toys "R" Us, Dollar General, TJMaxx, Marshall's, Tuesday Morning, Target, Wal-Mart (and so on), thrift stores, and library branches. See Chapters13 & 14 for ideas of where to find inventory.
- Find out about local book sales by calling your library branches or looking at their Friends sites online, checking out newspapers and looking at sites like these: Book Sale Finder: www.booksalefinder.com, Book Sale Manager: www.booksalemanager.com Book Sales Found: http://bit.ly/FREEtrialFrank
- Look for garage and estate sales.
- Note all local church/temple rummage sales in your calendar as they occur throughout the year – they'll occur about the same time again next year.

GLOSSARY

Amazon Buy Box - When you surf out to an item on Amazon.com, you usually see a price in red on the front page of that item. If you buy it with your "1-Click," you will buy it at that price. Approximately _70% of Amazon customers_ buy from the Buy Box. If you want to look at used or other offers, you have to click other links. Amazon uses a special algorithm for the Buy Box and cycles sellers through it based on price and whether or not they are FBA sellers (they get preference – another advantage for us). Generally, if you are within 3% of the lowest FBA price, you will get time in the Buy Box.

Amazon Prime - Another example of Amazon's brilliance is its Prime membership. If you are not a member of Prime, you should become one as soon as you can afford it. Being a Prime member gives you insight into your customer and is well worth the $79 a year. Basically, Prime members get free 2-day shipping on anything that Amazon sends out from its warehouse. They get overnight shipping for only $3.99. It is an awesome deal. They also can read 12 books a year free from Amazon's Kindle Lending Library and there are thousands of free movies they can download from Amazon for free. All those millions of people who have a (and who will get for Christmas!) Kindle Fire get a free trial membership. Believe me, no one turns it off after the trial. So what does this mean for us? Millions of new customers willing to pay a premium for our goods. Amazon has learned that the Prime member spends on average $500 _more_ a year on Amazon than the regular customer. Now you understand why they subsidize the Kindle and shipping costs for Prime members. They are locking in a customer for life.

ASIN - Amazon's unique 10-digit identifier for every product in its catalog, Amazon Standard Identification Number. Generally, Amazon includes UPC codes and ISBNs with each product as well. But, if there is no ISBN or UPC on your item, you can search for it on Amazon by name and then, under "product information" near the rank and other information, you will see the ASIN. You can copy and paste the ASIN into your listing program to bring up the data.

Bundle - A bundle is when you put two products together and sell them as one product. For example, one of my bundles is a cute bag container that attaches to a dog's leash and a supply of 150 poopy bags. I put the items into one bag together and created a unique listing on Amazon for this bundled product. Since I could not use the UPC code for either individual product, I bought a unique UPC code of my own. I buy them in batches and keep a spreadsheet of the code and what it matches on Amazon. It is very easy. The nice thing about bundles is you are the only seller for a while, maybe for always. It is a riskier proposition, and it can take a while before sales start going. In my case, my first bundle had 36 units and it took two years to sell them all. While my bundle was cute, the fact is there are a lot of poopy bags on Amazon and most dog owners are more interested in the bags than the leash carrying case. In that same two years, I sold hundreds of poopy bags without the case. If you are interested in pursuing bundles, think about what makes good gift items when you see them in the store – a popcorn maker with gourmet popcorn, for example.

Commingled/Stickerless - This is where your inventory is commingled with other inventory in the warehouse of the same kind and condition. When someone purchases an item from your inventory, Amazon doesn't physically distinguish your inventory from that of other merchants. The worker grabs a Barbie and fulfills the order. Your stock is decreased, of course. This is an option some sellers use for merchandise they are sending from a wholesaler directly to the warehouse, for example. It saves them the shipping and extra step of having to send the merchandise to their home, label it and re-ship it back out to Amazon. If the other merchants' items aren't as pristine as yours, however, your customers may get a dinged box and be unhappy with you. You have to weigh the convenience and cost against the potential risk.

FBA - Fulfillment by Amazon. Amazon's program that allows online sellers like us to leverage the logistical power and outstanding customer service of Amazon.com.

FNSKU - Amazon Fulfillment Network SKU (see MSKU below) is the unique identifier for each inventory item stored in one of Amazon's fulfillment centers. Amazon assigns this number to you after you list a product. The FNSKU is that strange mix of numbers and letters that prints on your label. It ties your Barbie doll, for example, to every detail about it like your MSKU, Amazon's ASIN, the UPC or ISBN, your price, your condition, your notes...everything.

Gross - The total amount of sales before any expenses are taken out. I sold over $40,000 worth of goods on Amazon my first year in business, but I took home less than that because of my expenses.

ISBN - This is the identifying number you'll find on or inside every book published after 1972. It stands for International Standard Book Number and is basically the UPC code for books. ISBNs can be 10 digits or (newer) 13 digits long. Some books will have both a 10-digit and a 13-digit number. If your book is pre-1972, you will need to look up the title on Amazon's website and grab the ASIN (see above) in order to list and sell the book on Amazon.

Long Tail - This is a phrase coined by Chris Anderson in the best-selling book *The Long Tail: Why the Future of Business is Selling Less of More*. This book dovetails neatly into Amazon's retail strategy of "selling everything on earth." The internet has made it possible for Amazon to exist and to sell millions upon millions of products. Anderson talks about the rise of the niche and how people distinguish themselves by their choices. When online sellers talk about a "Long-Tail Sale," they mean that their customer is rare and it may take a while to sell it, *but* the margin is sufficient to be worth the wait. Since it costs so little (relatively speaking – if the item is fairly small) to store stuff at Amazon, you can send in a book with a high margin and wait for it to sell. I did that with some books that I bought for $10 each and sold for $120 each, for example. It took a while for them to sell, but I felt confident there was an audience out there and the price was worth the wait.

Merchant Seller - Merchant sellers on Amazon fulfill their own inventory. These are the people you see selling a book for a penny. They are making their money on the shipping, basically. Merchants are also the people who sell their own merchandise on Amazon.com. A merchant seller may also be a retail store that is offering its goods on Amazon. I see this a lot with toys and health & beauty. Most customers prefer to buy from Amazon rather than a merchant seller. They are guaranteed fast shipping with the best customer service on the planet. If they want to return something after Christmas, they can do that easily and simply choose something else on Amazon.com to buy. Amazon makes it easy to ship back the unwanted item and the new item will be there in two days or less. If they buy from a merchant seller, they have to choose from the merchant's more limited inventory or wait to get their money back.It can take a couple of weeks. It's a hassle compared to Amazon.

MSKU - A merchant stock keeping unit (pronounced em-skew) is a fancy way of saying a unique number used to keep track of inventory. Each merchant (including us FBA sellers) needs to have a unique number that identifies the merchandise to ourselves, basically. ScanPower helps me generate an MSKU automatically. I customize it with details like the date and where I bought something. Months later when I'm looking at my inventory, I have a pretty good idea what it is, and I know how long it has been at Amazon. When I'm selling food, I add in the Best By date so I know at a glance when Amazon will be discarding my food. So far I've sold everything in plenty of time, but this way I can discount if I'm getting close to time.

Net - This is the number that remains after expenses are removed. When you get your check from Amazon, it is the net amount. Amazon removes all its commissions, fees and your shipping costs to the warehouse and gives you what is left. From that number, you would deduct your expenses like packing supplies, cost of inventory, etc., to get your profit.

Rank - This is a unique number that Amazon assigns to items based on the velocity of its sales. Amazon does not share its algorithm, so we don't know exactly how it is calculated. However, no two items in a category will have the same rank. There are no ties in Amazon's world. The lower the rank, the faster an item is selling. Rank basically tells you the last time something sold, *but not the next time it will sell*. If you see a book with a rank of 500,000, you know it sold something within the past week, but there's no guarantee it will sell something this week. Rank is very different from category to category. To give you perspective, a 500,000 in books is good because there are 32 million+ books in the category. In grocery which only has 755,000 items, a 500,000 would be pretty bad. I use rank as an indication that an item will sell on Amazon, but it is not the only factor I consider when I'm making a buying decision.

SKU - Stock Keeping Unit (pronounced skew) is used interchangeably with MSKU by most sellers although technically it is different. When you go to a store which has its own barcode that the checkout person scans, that's a SKU to you, but an MSKU to the store. In other words, an MSKU is owned by the merchant, a SKU is someone else's MSKU. (see MSKU above)

UPC Code - Universal Product Code. This is the manufacturer's number on a product usually in barcode form. It tells the whole world what it is. For example, a Tickle-Me-Elmo has the same UPC code whether it is in a Target or a Toys "R" Us. Amazon records the UPC code of every product on its product description page. When you scan the UPC code on an item, ScanPower (or whichever tool you use), uses that number to pull the data from the Amazon catalog. If a product has multiple versions, colors, sizes, etc., then your scanning tool may bring up multiple choices for you to pick from. This happens a lot with toys because they are often sold in mixed lots. For example, the UPC code may be for "Assorted Marvel Comic Heroes," and include a selection of hero action figures, not just one. If you are holding Thor in your hands, you want to pick the picture of Thor on your scanner from all the heroes that come up.

USB - Universal Serial Bus is a connection standard used by computers and other devices like smartphones, flash drives, cameras and more. Today, nearly all connections to your computer like the Dymo printer and the handheld USB scanner I recommend will have a cord with a USB plug at one end that goes into a matching port on your computer or laptop.

Seller Central - This is the health monitor of your Amazon business. It is live and up-to-date with your inventory, sales, net check (my favorite vital sign!), customer correspondence, reporting and much, much, more. It is overwhelming at first, but as you get familiar with all the data Amazon keeps for you, you will love it. If you ever wonder "does Amazon do XYZ for me?" the answer is probably yes! We even have our own seller support team at Amazon who will help you navigate Seller Central and find the answers to your questions. Be aware that if you are currently an individual seller, when you upgrade to Pro, your Seller Central will be much bigger and much more. You'll need to take time to learn what is new because there will be a lot that is new and/or different for Pro sellers.

Smartphone - Any phone that has a sophisticated operating system and a large touch-screen, basically. To run most scanning programs, you need a smartphone with a minimum of 3G (4G is preferred for fastest look-ups), an unlimited or very high data plan (I have 2 GB a month with AT&T which I never used up until my teenage son joined my plan) and either the Android or Apple operating system. Android phones are open system phones that run on open, shared software developed by Google. iPhones are created by Apple. I've used both types of phones and they are excellent. Android phones are less expensive.

ABOUT THE AUTHOR

Cynthia Stine has 25+ years of strategic consulting, PR/ marketing, business development and communications experience that has included launching dozens of companies and bringing literally hundreds of products to market in such diverse industries as high technology, data communications, Internet, telecommunications, retail, consumer goods, energy, healthcare and financial services. She has worked with both public and private companies and helped several venture-funded companies achieve successful IPOs through strategic communications. She's launched such technologies as the world's first pen-based computer, DSL technology, VOIP and the world's first flywheel battery.

She has owned her own business since 1994 including PRTek, a high-tech public relations agency she sold in 2001; PUBLISH for Success, an independent publisher of non-fiction books sold to a partner in 2006; Promote Success, a full-service PR firm in Dallas; and MyPromote Books, a book consulting and publishing firm which also sells books and other products on Amazon through its used book division.

During her career, Cynthia has consistently served as a mentor to other small business owners. She strongly believes that the future workforce will increasingly consist of self-directed individuals working collaboratively rather than a traditional big-company command-and-control infrastructure.

It is natural, then, that she would be drawn to online sales where a small fish can carve up its piece of a big pond and where working collaboratively ensures greater prosperity for all.

If you would like to talk with Cynthia about your Amazon business, she offers several training and consulting options to help get you started. She is also a public speaker if you would like her to speak to your group.

Learn more at: http://www.sellstepbystep.com.